ENDORSEMENTS

In this age of social media, Facebook has become an extraordinarily powerful gatekeeper of information and a severely irresponsible one, relentlessly censoring conservatives and voices of freedom, and running interference for the left and Islamic supremacists, most notoriously in blocking criticism of Europe's suicidal immigration and refugee policies. As Joe Newby and Adina Kutnicki show in this unique and essential book, we can't get word out about any serious initiative these days without Facebook, but Facebook is wholly in thrall to the left. In *BANNED: How Facebook Enables Militant Islamic Jihad*, Newby and Kutnicki reveal the shocking truth of just how deep the corruption goes and details a cohesive and workable plan for how defenders of freedom can gain and preserve a voice on this essential social media platform.

— PAMELA GELLER, PRESIDENT, AMERICAN FREEDOM DEFENSE
INITIATIVE AND AUTHOR OF THE POST-AMERICAN PRESIDENCY:
THE OBAMA ADMINISTRATION'S WAR ON AMERICA

BANNED: How Facebook Enables Militant Islamic Jihad will astonish you. *BANNED* is co-authored by American-Israeli Adina Kutnicki, an investigative journalist and expert on the Muslim Brotherhood, and by Joe Newby, a 10-year veteran of the United States Marine Corps, who is also an investigative journalist.

Kutnicki, who immigrated to Israel in 2008, is well connected with Israeli opinion makers and has become one of Israel's most acute political analysts.

Newby, co-author of *BANNED*, is an internet specialist whose own articles appear on a variety of conservative sites including LibertyUnyielding.com. Kutnicki, living in Israel, has uncensored knowledge of the genocidal aims of the Palestinian Authority (PA). The PA is the Palestinian wing of the Muslim Brotherhood, whose global objectives are being implemented throughout Islamdom and with the blessings of the Muslim penetrated administration of US President Barack Obama.

As the coauthors of *BANNED*, Kutnicki and Newby can prove through documented evidence, exhibits, and a fully footnoted discussion of the subject matter, how FACEBOOK, along with other primary social media sites, magnifies the anti-Western influence of imperialistic Islam.

Indeed, the primary focus of the Kutnicki-Newby revelations are the socio-political dangers that Facebook, as a covert carrier of Islamism, poses to America and Israel, the main pillars of Western Civilization, or of what's left of it.

Kutnicki and Newby show in *BANNED* that these enemies obscure their sinister designs by hypocritical professions of peace, pluralism, and democracy, while marching to the drum beat of jihadic Islam. *BANNED* is must reading.

—PROFESSOR PAUL EIDELBERG (PHD, UNIVERSITY OF CHICAGO) IS AN AMERICAN-ISRAELI POLITICAL SCIENTIST, AUTHOR AND LECTURER, AND IS THE FOUNDER AND PRESIDENT OF THE FOUNDATION FOR CONSTITUTIONAL DEMOCRACY, WITH OFFICES IN JERUSALEM. HE IS THE AUTHOR OF OVER 21 BOOKS, INCLUDING A TRILOGY ON AMERICA'S FOUNDING FATHERS: THE PHILOSOPHY OF THE AMERICAN CONSTITUTION, ON THE SILENCE OF THE DECLARATION OF INDEPENDENCE, AND A DISCOURSE ON STATESMANSHIP.

In the decades between the first two world wars, a storm was brewing in the minds of angry Islamic thinkers who could not contain their fury over the fall of the Caliphate. Out of the thunder and lightning of that angry defeat, the Muslim Brotherhood was born. Dedicated to restoring the Caliphate and imposing Islam with its Sharia Law on the entire human race, the modern Islamist movement emerged, and with it, the clash of civilizations that may lead to a third world war.

Fast-forward 90 years, and we have a world plagued by dozens of Islamic terror organizations sowing death on every continent, and yet, the so-called leaders of the Free World refuse to even use the word *Islam* in the same sentence as the word *terror*. The suicide bombers and mass murderers, with their solid foundation in Islam and Jew-hate based on the Islamic ideology of Muslim Brotherhood theorist Sayyid Qutb, quote the Qur'an, the Hadith, and Sharia law chapter and verse to justify their actions while Western leaders claim the terrorists are common criminals, not Muslims.

Adina Kutnicki has been confronting this bizarre, through-the-looking glass world of Muslim Brotherhood-inspired political Islam and the denial of the West in her work as an author and investigative journalist for more than a decade. On her blog, in articles that have appeared in numerous international publications, and in several groundbreaking, no-holds-barred interviews with American mainstream media, Adina has documented the danger that every single non-Muslim alive today is facing from political Islam.

Ms. Kutnicki understands the essential role the Brotherhood, the titular head of militant Islamic Jihad, plays in establishing an all-important political base for Islamists to build upon. A base that allows them to deny involvement with terrorism, while they channel funds to Islamist killers and take over nations. Yet the West continues to ignore the truth; Europe is overrun, and Obama imports unvetted Muslims from the Middle East's hotbed of Jihad by the thousands.

If you care about your future, and you wish to live in a world that respects human rights and personal freedom, you must educate yourself on the enemy we are all facing, and that enemy is political Islam. I would suggest that this book, *BANNED: How Facebook Enables Militant Islamic Jihad*, is the best place to start. Adina Kutnicki and Joe Newby will give you the facts, the details and the background you will need to prepare for a world that is rapidly approaching the breaking point through the assistance of various enablers and their collaborative efforts. After all, the Muslim Brotherhood is quite happy to tell you what their goals are, even if men like Obama, Trudeau, and Cameron, and women like Merkel and Clinton are happy to lie to our faces.

Finally, do you want Facebook to decide whether or not militant Islamic Jihadists deserve safe spaces within civilized society, as they lay out the welcome mat at their site? Do you want to live under a Caliphate with Islam the only permitted religion and Sharia law replacing your secular Constitution? If you don't, start reading on page one."

–WOLFF BACHNER, HEAD EDITOR INQUISITR.COM, A HIGHLY POPULAR NEWS WEBSITE WITH MILLIONS OF READERS. WOLFF IS ALSO A RESPECTED POLITICAL COLUMNIST WITH A FOCUS ON THE MIDDLE EAST, RELIGIOUS EXTREMISM, REGULATORY ISSUES AND PERSONAL FREEDOM. WOLFF HAS INTERVIEWED MANY OF ISRAEL'S LEADING JOURNALISTS, POLITICAL FIGURES AND SECURITY EXPERTS. WHEN HE ISN'T COVERING THE LATEST POLITICAL CRISIS, WOLFF DEVOTES HIS ENERGIES TO EXPOSING THE EXPANSIONIST IDEOLOGIES OF MODERN ISLAM, AND THE 1,400-YEARS-LONG HISTORY OF RAMPANT JEW-HATE FOUND IN ISLAMIC DOGMA AND DOCTRINE.

BANNED:

How Facebook Enables Militant Islamic Jihad

BANNED:

How Facebook Enables Militant Islamic Jihad

ADINA KUTNICKI
AND
JOE NEWBY

BANNED:

Copyright © 2016 by Adina Kutnicki and Joe Newby

World Ahead Press is a division of WND Books. The views and opinions expressed in this book are those of the authors and do not necessarily reflect the official policy or position or WND Books.

Paperback ISBN: 978-1-944212-22-3
eBook ISBN: 978-1-944212-23-0

Printed in the United States of America
16 17 18 19 20 21 LSI 9 8 7 6 5 4 3 2 1

It is to you, my sons, that I dedicate this book. I am forever grateful for your loving and generous hearts. You are the lights of my life, as are your precious little ones. It will be through continuous vigilance, sacrifice, and the perseverance of patriots that the twin pillars of western civilization, America and Israel, stand strong. This is my fervent hope and prayer. To said end, I dedicate my efforts.

—ADINA KUTNICKI

To Wendy, my lovely bride of thirty years who has stood by my side through thick and thin, in good times and bad, you are forever the love of my life; to her parents, Cliff and Lorraine, for their many years of love and support; to the memory of my dad, Merle; to my children, Mishia and Rick, and to my grandchildren, with hopes they will inherit a safe, free and prosperous world.

—JOE NEWBY

If not us, who? If not now, when?

— HILLEL THE ELDER (110 BC—10 AD)

"The further a society drifts from the truth, the more it will hate those that speak it."

— GEORGE ORWELL

"If you know the enemy and know yourself, you need not fear the result of a hundred battles. If you know yourself but not the enemy, for every victory gained you will also suffer a defeat. If you know neither the enemy nor yourself, you will succumb in every battle."

— SUN TZU (CIRCA 544–496 BC) THE ART OF WAR

CONTENTS

FOREWORD

The book before you is written by two acknowledged experts, one of whom is deeply immersed in exposing militant Islamic jihad, the other in investigating the little known underbelly of the largest social media site on the planet.

I have worked with investigative journalist and blogger Adina Kutnicki for a good number of years, and have relied upon her wealth of knowledge and network of contacts to alert Americans and Israelis (westerners at large) to the greatest threat level bar none, Islamic terrorism. So much so, I share with her information which is both sensitive and explosive. Without hesitation or reservation, her dedication to the cause of uncovering the network of Islamic terrorism and its front groups is unsurpassed. It is for this reason that I devoted one of my newsletter articles on Islamic based terrorism intelligence with the headline: Adina Kutnicki: Hero For America and Israel.

And it was after completing intelligence gathering at one of the many conferences sponsored by the Muslim Brotherhood Mafia (through its intricate network of front groups) within America, having conveyed my findings to Adina Kutnicki, that she introduced me to Joe Newby, an expert on Facebook.

Most alarmingly, while undercover, it was discovered that Facebook works alongside the Brotherhood to help present a more *benign* face of Islam to Americans and the west. Notably, Facebook representatives are operating in tandem with CAIR (Council on American-Islamic Relations), their U.S. based propaganda arm.

It is impossible to overstate the magnitude of the threat, that which reaches an unprecedented level when considering the net effect of CAIR (and related Sunni Brotherhood arms) co-joining with Facebook.

Most Americans, Israelis, and westerners truly view Facebook (like an array of social media sites) as a forum to catch up with old friends, make new ones, connect with relatives near and far, and to engage in virtual exchanges of information. This is all well and good. However, an increasing number of Islamic terrorists are duly versed in technology and its usage for jihad and related tasks, paradoxically, even though their main mission is to revert the world back to centuries ago. Their aim is to bring about a world Caliphate which is in line with Muhammad, the Islamic prophet. As a key component to their global ambitions, their leadership understands that exploiting the core internal weaknesses of America and the west - obsessively fixated on multiculturalism and the fear of criticizing anything related to Islam - is central and mandatory.

By and large, the revelations contained within this well researched, thoroughly detailed and amply exhibited book portends the following danger: The convergence of efforts between the Muslim Brotherhood Mafia's surrogates and Facebook (alongside other heavy-lifters) should be considered a force multiplier with untold ramifications. For when the world's largest and most dangerous Islamic terror organization is able to enlist the assistance (on any level, be it primary or second-tier) of the biggest social media site on the planet, let there be no doubt that Facebook has chosen sides, whether announced or hidden from public view.

Conclusively, freedom-loving people have a duty to speak truth to power, while they still can. This is precisely where the value of this book lies, in so far that America, as the leader of the west, is teetering on the edge of censorship, all the while more and more citizens are self-censoring due to PC infiltration into major spheres of influence. In no uncertain terms, Facebook, in unseen ways, is a big part of this insidious silencing.

My heartfelt thanks to Adina Kutnicki, an American (and Israeli) patriot, and Joe Newby, a former Marine Corps veteran, for exposing Facebook as a tool of Islamic terrorism.

—DAVE GAUBATZ, FORMER SPECIAL AGENT WITH THE UNITED STATES AIR FORCE OFFICE OF SPECIAL INVESTIGATIONS (AFOSI). MR. GAUBATZ HAS WORKED COUNTERINTELLIGENCE AND COUNTERTERRORISM STATESIDE AS WELL AS IN SEVERAL MIDDLE EASTERN COUNTRIES. MR. GAUBATZ WAS THE FIRST US CIVILIAN FEDERAL AGENT DEPLOYED TO IRAQ WHEN OPERATION IRAQI FREEDOM BEGAN. ARMED WITH THE HIGHEST SECURITY CLEARANCES (TOP SECRET/SCI), HE HAS BEEN BRIEFED INTO SEVERAL BLACK PROJECTS. OVER THE PAST SEVERAL YEARS HE HAS BEEN CONDUCTING INTELLIGENCE INSIDE AMERICA, ZEROING IN ON THE VAST NETWORK OF SAUDI-BACKED TERROR MOSQUES AND BROTHERHOOD NETWORKS EMBEDDED WITHIN THE HIGHEST ECHELONS OF THE NATION. MR. GAUBATZ IS ALSO THE AUTHOR OF MUSLIM MAFIA: INSIDE THE SECRET UNDERWORLD THAT'S CONSPIRING TO ISLAMIZE AMERICA.

ACKNOWLEDGMENTS

It is to my beloved husband, Frank Kutnicki, of blessed memory, I owe the most. **He was incomparable, one in a million**. His booming laughter still resonates in my heart and mind's eye. He brought me immeasurable joy. His unique ability to treat others kindly still serves as my guiding example. Ever so gently, he softened my sharp edges. Simply put, he made me a more compassionate person. He uplifted me. He quietly walks beside me every day, strengthening me, so that I can continue living a life filled with love, all the while fighting our righteous western struggle.

To my dear parents, Irene Silverman Dzikansky and Rabbi Jekuthiel Dzikansky, of blessed memory, who taught me that riches are not measured by material wealth, rather by how one lives life, honestly and with integrity. In the Jewish text, *Ethics of The Fathers*: Chapter Four, it is written: "Who is rich? One who is satisfied with his lot." This remains forever in my heart.

Not to be remiss, a heartfelt thanks to my valued contacts - even to those not mentioned - all of whom are top notch professionals. None of my work would be possible without their *specialized* assistance. Most notably:

To Dave Gaubatz, how can I adequately describe your heroism and service to America's security, other than to say: I am in awe! You embody the true character traits of a patriot. I am humbled to be considered a confidante, as well as a loyal friend. You emerged "from the shadows" through your investigative book, *Muslim Mafia: Inside the Secret Underworld That's Conspiring to Islamize America*. Americans, westerners alike, owe you a profound debt.

To Wolff Bachner, a top-tier editor-in-chief, your incisive knowledge base of geo-politics often helps to contextualize rapidly shifting patterns of conflict. You are without peer as an interviewer.

To Professor Louis René Beres, you are rightfully considered a world-class expert on nuclear terrorism, strategy and international law. Even so, you always, ever so patiently, took the time to answer - over the years - my many questions on the most crucial issues of our time. You are a gentleman and a scholar. Thank you for being my *mentor.*

To Professor Paul Eidelberg, you are a true Renaissance man, an exemplar of what it means to be both an American and Israeli patriot. A first-class political scientist, you enriched my depth of the subject matter immeasurably. Not only that, your core understanding of Islamic politics, history, culture and religious-based imperatives have been invaluable. Not to be forgotten, your insights into Judaism's Biblical texts have been very incisive. I am beyond grateful.

To Dr. Martin Sherman, you taught me how to tune out the incessant chatter from Israel's non-elected *elitists*, thus, zeroing in on the most intrinsic - and often multi-pronged - strategic imperatives at hand. Unarguably, you are Israel's foremost strategic policy analyst.

Last, but certainly not least, to those who have been instrumental in keeping me in the loop, a special shout out, as you courageously operate in the murky and dangerous field of counterterrorism. To my American contacts John L., Dan S., Bob Z., and Steve F. To my Israeli contacts Rami A., "Dudu" N., Asaf T., "Shuki" A., and "Tommy" L. For obvious reasons, your anonymity must remain in place.

G-dspeed to America, Israel, and the west in toto.

INTRODUCTION

While militant jihad is exploding throughout the west, within Islamic dominated nations alike, as they engage in their centuries-long struggle for Sunni versus Shia hegemony – increasingly, non-Muslim westerners who refuse to bow to the dictates of Islam are subjected to gravely perilous circumstances. The proofs are beyond manifest. Most visibly, they can be seen through militant jihad's bloody swathe across the world. Irrefutable.

Not only that, in *polite* society it is verboten to dissect the underpinnings of the Qur'an which are derived from the *teachings* of Muhammad. Inarguably, he was a pedophile, rapist, pilferer, sadist and a clinical psychopath. The urgent question becomes: why is delving into the pathology of Adolf Hitler (in general, history's mass murderers) deemed a scholarly exercise, yet, it is clearly forbidden, let alone inextricably dangerous, to question the sanity of the *prophet* of a billion plus followers? Is this omertà even rational, let alone acceptable?

And it is not as if the aforementioned is without substantive basis and merit. Consequently, it has been a focal point of this author's work-product. In tandem, others (with inquiring minds) have executed considerable heavy-lifting, and the following excerpts are supportive of the same:

> *The fundamental problem of Islam is the belief that God talked to Muhammad and dictated the contents of the Koran to him. Muslims are indoctrinated into believing the Koran is God's word, and so they act on the numerous incitements to violence that they find in it.*

19

What they find in the Koran came from the mind of Muhammad, and for insight into the mental condition of this "prophet," consider Chapter 33 of his Koran, entitled "The Confederates." This is one of the chapters Muhammad composed in Yathrib (later called Medina) where he fled after his Meccan compatriots realized they needed to kill him to preserve their way of life.

The chapter is like a wild theme park ride that races in and out of numerous topics. In the 73 verses that make up the chapter, Muhammad covers the following in the God-voice he used for the Koran: He recaps a recent battle with the Meccans and excoriates people who were afraid to fight and die for him; he gloats about his extermination of the men and boys of one of the Jewish tribes of Yathrib, the confiscation of their property, and the enslavement of their women and children; he authorizes himself to take as many wives as he likes, permits himself to marry the wife of his adopted son, forbids himself from taking any more wives after he has taken as many as he likes, but allows himself sex slaves.

As the verses of this "revelation" continue, Muhammad imposes full body and face cover for women when outside the home, threatens people with humiliating punishment in the afterlife for annoying him, threatens to murder his critics, prohibits the practice of adoption, and dishes up images of sadistic torture in Hell awaiting people who don't believe in him. He also praises himself as a "lamp spreading light," and holds his behavior as a "beautiful pattern" for people to follow if they want to score well with Allah.

Among the verses is a celestial advisory that he must be obeyed:

"It is not fitting for a Believer, man or woman, when a matter has been decided by Allah and His Messenger to have any option about their decision: if any one disobeys Allah and His Messenger, he is indeed on a clearly wrong Path." (Koran 33:36) [All of the Koran quotes in this article are taken from the Yusuf

Ali translation.] . . .

More self-praise can be found in Verse 56 wherein he advises believers to bless him and "salute him with all respect," because that is what Allah and Allah's angels do to him.

This is followed by a suite of verses that rail against people who refuse to believe that God talks to him, salutes him, and blesses him. He threatens infidels that they will pay for their lack of belief in him in blazing hellfire. "Our Lord! Give them double Penalty and curse them with a very great Curse!" he says in Verse 68.

The Koran is full of such nonsense and oozes with Muhammad's hatred for people who rejected him. But it is not necessary to read the entire book to realize it is the product on an extremely disturbed mind.

Islam is demented because it is all about Muhammad and his claim that God talked to him. His delusion of communion with the divine was likely brought about by epileptic fits caused by a malformed temporal lobe. He was a psychopath as well, a lethal combination that led him down the path of pathological evil.

Islam represents the institutionalized version of his neurological and psychological disorders.

All you have to do to understand the truth about the mind that created Islam and the ideology that is threatening the world is to read Chapter 33 of Muhammad's Koran, which means "Recital."

It is the recital of a madman. [1]

Thus, it is into this vortex of hell that social media has managed to attain and assert its prominence, and to an exponential degree. Inherently, it is through social media platforms that jihadists comfortably congregate, *friend* like-minded Islamists, message, plot, and ultimately *inspire* one another to wage global jihad.

In this regard, it is not accidental, nor incidental, that al-Qaeda in the Arabian Peninsula's (the jihadi group which spawned ISIS, both of which are integrally linked to the Muslim Brotherhood) slick high profile glossy propaganda magazine is entitled *Inspire*. Effectively, in so far as millions upon millions can potentially reach out to fellow jihadists through a few clicks, the sky is the limit.

Most significantly, Facebook is their go - to forum, even though Twitter and others are part and parcel of said phenomena. Alas, jihadists are warmly welcomed and embraced within Facebook's family, as will be proven through a compendium of work by the authors of this book. On the other side of the spectrum, heaven forfend, if one espouses patriotic and conservative ethos. More specifically, if one's perspective leans in the direction of a pro-American stance - evinced through an ideologically and socially conservative bent circle of *friends*, who, for the most part, are staunchly Judeo-Christian in nature - well, the hammer at Facebook hits hardest – Boom! Not only that, a double *crime* is committed in said arena, that is, if one dares to hold steadfast to both pro-American and pro-Israel ideology and concomitant support thereof - *BANNED*!

It is due to the above, and so much more, that it became an absolute imperative to compile this book. Now, experts are few and far between in the combined arenas of investigative journalism, geopolitics, and Islam's relationship to militant jihad. To wit, it is incumbent upon all of us to share our wealth of knowledge, as well as our experiences. It is along this treacherous minefield that a double-edged sword evolves; exploding dangers from militant jihad, in tandem with a continuous struggle to fend off assaults from the likes of Facebook's denizens and arbiters of what is considered acceptable online discourse *a la* its ubiquitous rules of conduct.

With over 1.6 billion users worldwide, Facebook is clearly the largest social media site on the planet. For all practical purposes, Facebook has become the *de facto* Internet since nearly every site connects to it in one form or another. With that size comes great power, the power to lift up and the power to destroy. CEO Mark

Zuckerberg has been caught on an open microphone promising to stifle negative stories of migrants and he recently promised the world's Muslims to make his site an open and welcoming place for them.

But as we will illustrate, the company has already been doing that. In the process, it has falsely accused many users, banning them from certain features on the flimsiest of contrived *evidence*, and has torn down pages over patently false claims and claims that are questionable at best. Many of these actions have caused financial losses, but it seems America's legal profession has been cowed into acquiescence by the company's sheer size.

We frequently hear politicians speak of companies not being too big to fail. But is Facebook too big to be regulated? Is Facebook so big that it can freely operate as a government unto itself?

A couple of final notes are in order here. First, despite what some detractors may say, this book is not about individual Muslims. We recognize that not all Muslims believe in the concept of militant jihad, and are impacted by Facebook's actions as well. We do provide a discussion of militant jihad to provide context and give you, the reader, a better understanding of the overall problem. It is, however, about how the largest social media site on the planet seems to give preferential treatment to one group of people at the expense of everyone else. Second, the reader should know that we reached out to Facebook in an effort to give them an opportunity to discuss and explain the incidents mentioned in this book. So far, the company has not responded.

PART I – DEFINING THE PROBLEM

CHAPTER ONE

THE FACEBOOK PROBLEM

Imagine for a moment sitting down to your computer to check the day's messages and catch up on what has been happening in your favorite Facebook pages. You go to Facebook and suddenly get hit with a notice that you've been logged out and need to log back in. You do, only to discover that something you supposedly wrote or posted violated Facebook's Community Standards.

You scratch your head wondering when you made the post, but click "Okay" and are suddenly told that you've been banned from posting for thirty days. Congratulations. You've just been placed into *Facebook Jail,* and have joined the ranks of many millions of others.

Facebook, no doubt the single largest social media site on the planet with well over 1.6 billion registered users worldwide, has a stringent and somewhat nebulous set of standards that are supposed to guide, and in theory, protect the user. Standards and guidelines are necessary in order to keep the site from devolving into chaos and anarchy.

Most don't have a problem with guidelines or standards, but problems can and do arise when those standards are not enforced objectively. And it doesn't take much to violate those rules. Just say the wrong thing in a comment or post a picture someone doesn't like and you're almost certain to end up in Facebook's doghouse.

One of the topics that gets many users slapped is Islam. Make a post critical of Islam, especially Islamic jihad, and Facebook's moderators are certain to spring into action.

Many users have experienced Facebook's wrath and many pages have been repeatedly unpublished, sometimes over claims and *evidence* made up out of whole cloth. This would seem to fly in the face of a statement made by CEO Mark Zuckerberg shortly after the 2015 *Charlie Hebdo* attack in Paris.

"Facebook has always been a place where people across the world share their views and ideas. We follow the laws in each country, but we never let one country or group of people dictate what people can share across the world," he wrote on his own timeline. "Yet as I reflect on yesterday's attack and my own experience with extremism, this is what we all need to reject—a group of extremists trying to silence the voices and opinions of everyone else around the world." The next sentence is key, "I won't let that happen on Facebook. I'm committed to building a service where you can speak freely without fear of violence."[1]

It would seem that Zuckerberg is actually expressing support for the expression of different opinions, even those he disagrees with. But just eight months later, he was caught on an open microphone telling German Chancellor Angela Merkel that he was working on ways to stifle negative stories about migrants. "The Facebook CEO was overheard responding that 'we need to do some work' on curtailing anti-immigrant posts about the refugee crisis," CNBC reported at the time. "'Are you working on this?' Merkel asked in English, to which Zuckerberg replied in the affirmative before the transmission was disrupted."[2]

Did Zuckerberg have a change of heart? Did he really mean what he said in January, or was it just an emotional response to a horrific event? In January, he shared with the world that he was threatened with a death sentence for not banning posts critical of the Islamic prophet Muhammad. Did that guide his statement to Merkel?

Fast-forward about three or four months when news broke of a damning video produced by Shurat HaDin, the Israel Law Center, an organization that has filed a massive class action lawsuit against Facebook. For perhaps the first time, the social media giant's tendency to favor Islam was documented for the whole world to see.

In that experiment, Shurat HaDin set up two nearly identical pages, one critical of Israel and the Jews, and another critical of Palestine. Nearly identical posts were made on each page attacking the other side. The posts became more provocative as time went on. Finally, both pages were reported to see how Facebook would respond. Predictably, the pro-Israel page was yanked while the pro-Palestinian page remained live. Facebook finally removed the other page, but only after its bias was exposed on video.[3]

More damning, with unabashed arrogance, the following was noted by one of its research scientists in a post entitled, *Facebook Tweaks Algorithm to Lower Click-Bait Posts*. Facebook is on a quest to weed out links to click-baiting stories that are designed to make people click on them. The social network says that by monitoring how long people spend reading news articles, as well as how they interact with them, it can prioritize the best content that pops up in people's news feeds.

In a blog post, research scientist Khalid El-Arini, and Joyce Tang, a product specialist at Facebook, said the firm has made improvements, "to help people find the posts and links from publishers that are most interesting and relevant, and to continue to weed out stories that people frequently tell us are spammy and that they don't want to see. Facebook said a survey revealed that 80 percent of its users prefer headlines what make the content of an article crystal clear, so they can work out if a link is worth clicking on."[4]

This bias, as we will demonstrate in this book, also extends to individuals who write about the topic of Islamic jihad and regular users, some of whom have received very disturbing and explicit threats of violence and death. And as we will illustrate, this problem has plagued Facebook users since at least 2010.

Not only that, what are we to make of an entity which refused to remove a page exhorting to assassinate Donald Trump? Are we to assume that since *The Donald* is not bending leftward, nor in Islam's (prostrating) direction, that he deserves to be murdered? Truly, is this considered acceptable practice by Facebook? Moreover, does it meet with their self-professed rigorous standards of conduct? Mind you, is it even tolerable (not to mention, it rises to criminal conduct) within any civilized society, no less? Readers, you decide.

"While censoring posts mildly critical of feminism, Facebook has refused to remove a page entitled "Assassinate Donald Trump," claiming that it doesn't violate the company's 'community standards'."[5] After a Facebook user reported the page, Facebook responded by saying it would take no further action.

"We reviewed the Page you reported for having a credible threat of violence and found it doesn't violate our 'Community Standards,' states the message. While open calls to assassinate a presidential candidate are apparently fine, Facebook takes a much harsher stance when it comes to criticism of radical feminism."[5] Head-spinning. Mind-numbing. Wretched. Criminal. Uncivilized. Feel free to fill in the blanks. Still yet, to be overly generous, no one is accusing Facebook of actively supporting or funding militant Islamic jihad. It doesn't need to. Its actions, comparable to those of the lazy parent who refuses to acknowledge the bad behavior of his or her children, enable militant jihad and ultimately put people's lives in danger.

Hyperbole? Hardly. The situation has gotten so bad that Amos Yadlin, a former head of the Israel Defense Forces Military Intelligence Directorate and the current executive director of the Tel Aviv-based Institute for National Security Studies, said that the "The most dangerous nation in the Middle East acting against Israel is the state of Facebook . . . " He further states, "It has a lot more power than anybody who's operating an armed force," and, "Unlike before, there's no longer an existential military threat facing Israel. Rather, it's a strategic threat." [6]

To understand the totality of the problem, the reader needs to have a basic understanding of militant Islamic jihad, which is far more complex than most really know.

CHAPTER TWO

MILITANT JIHAD:
ITS KNOCK-ON EFFECTS TO THE WEST

Very soon after September 11, 2001, militant jihad, seemingly out of nowhere, catapulted into the lives of each and every American. Forthwith, mega shock waves reverberated within the nation as well as throughout the world. Many Americans were left dumbfounded and shell-shocked, asking questions which fixated alongside the same theme: How could this happen? What did we do wrong? And what does this mean for the future?

While these queries were more than valid within the context of September 11, 2001, and its immediate aftermath, those of us steeped in the whys and wherefores of militant jihad and its inextricable relationship to Islam, were more outraged than shocked. And even that is a bit of an understatement.

On the other hand, most Americans were forced to familiarize themselves with the bloody reality and consequences of militant jihad, even though the preponderance of citizens had no idea about the ins and outs of the encircling dangers. Tragically, almost fifteen years onward, many still remain in the dark and are comfortable being blind as bats. And regardless of where one stood on the *shock barometer* right after September 11, 2001, the fact of the matter is that its knock-on effects were rippling inside America, and well before that fateful day, albeit, under the radar.

In reality, the *opening shot of jihad* on United States soil made its official debut on November 5, 1990, with the very brazen public assassination of Rabbi Meir Kahane at the New York Marriott East Side Hotel in Manhattan, New York. Its basis was expounded upon in an op-ed at Israel National News (in 2005) by one of the co-authors. The following is an excerpt:

> *Fifteen years after Rabbi Kahane's murder, National Geographic, much to their credit, finally connected the most undeniable and intrinsic dot in their very well-documented four-part series entitled* Inside 9/11. *The focus of their documentary was on a timeline of Islamic jihad against the US. Lo and behold, they concluded, much like Kahane's supporters, that Rabbi Kahane's assassination was the opening of jihad on US soil. This documentary was deemed so important and so relevant that it was made available free of charge to those areas that do not have access to the* National Geographic *cable channel.*[1]

Not only that, Israel has been battling militant jihad, that is, the very same scourge from *time immemorial*, long before its rebirth as a modern state in 1948. Intrinsically, this tiny sliver of land should be considered a "laboratory" for America and the west at large, in relationship to what works and what doesn't. In point of fact, so much so, after September 11, 2001, Raymond W. Kelly, the NYPD's Police Commissioner and the most proactive and results-oriented police commissioner in the US to date, reacted thusly:

> *Leave it to the out-of-the-box thinking of the head of the NYPD (New York Police Department) to come to the rescue, at least as far as securing New York City, to a degree unprecedented in law enforcement. To this end, after witnessing the horrific attacks of 9/11/01, Police Commissioner Raymond W. Kelly decided to take the offensive, not satisfied to leave New York City's counterterror activities to the Feds. He (rightfully) concluded that sharing intelligence was not their strong suit, as layers of obstacles exist between the many competing agencies. Commissioner Kelly*

instinctively realized that time was of the essence and that he had to act. And act he did.

Therefore, he put into effect New York City's first ever Counter Terror Unit, operating both inside New York City and outside its borders. In a particularly brilliant strategic move, he also decided to station several of New York City's best detectives at overseas posts, sites chosen based on their levels of Islamic terror activity.

To wit, from 2003 through the beginning of 2008, Detective Mordecai "Morty" Dzikansky, Homicide Detective, First Grade, was sent to the first ever posting in Tel Aviv, Israel. His task was to set up shop, interface (with the Israeli National Police), collect intel, and otherwise react to terror events as they occurred.

Much to his credit, Commissioner Kelly understood that to learn from the experts how best to fight Islamic terrorists necessitated sending one of New York's finest to the best laboratory in the world – Israel.[2]

Even so, in order to fully internalize the grave dangers embedded within militant jihad, its knock-on effects to western civilization, it is imperative to commence with a *working* definition, one which grabs onto its root(s) and core. In reality, not only must it be understood for what it is, but for what it isn't.

Effectively, it is efficacious to start with what it isn't, in so far as America, Israel and the wider west are concerned. To be clear, jihad, at its base, is explained away by western apologists through a well-worn definition propagated by Islamists. In brief, according to The Islamic Supreme Council of America:

WHAT JIHAD IS

- *The Arabic word "jihad" is often translated as "holy war," but in a purely linguistic sense, the word " jihad" means struggling or striving.*

- *The arabic word for war is: "al-harb".*

- *In a religious sense, as described by the Qur'an and teachings of the Prophet Muhammad (s), "jihad" has many meanings. It can refer to internal as well as external efforts to be a good Muslims or believer, as well as working to inform people about the faith of Islam.*

- *If military jihad is required to protect the faith against others, it can be performed using anything from legal, diplomatic and economic to political means. If there is no peaceful alternative, Islam also allows the use of force, but there are strict rules of engagement. Innocents - such as women, children, or invalids - must never be harmed, and any peaceful overtures from the enemy must be accepted.*

- *Military action is therefore only one means of jihad, and is very rare. To highlight this point, the Prophet Mohammed told his followers returning from a military campaign: "This day we have returned from the minor jihad to the major jihad," which he said meant returning from armed battle to the peaceful battle for self-control and betterment.*

- *In case military action appears necessary, not everyone can declare jihad. The religious military campaign has to be declared by a proper authority, advised by scholars, who say the religion and people are under threat and violence is imperative to defend them. The concept of "just war" is very important.*

- *The concept of jihad has been hijacked by many political and religious groups over the ages in a bid to justify various forms of violence. In most cases, Islamic splinter groups invoked jihad to fight against the established Islamic order. Scholars say this misuse of jihad contradicts Islam.*

- *Examples of sanctioned military jihad include the Muslims' defensive battles against the Crusaders in medieval times, and before that some responses by Muslims against Byzantine and Persian attacks during the period of the early Islamic conquests.*

WHAT JIHAD IS NOT

- *Jihad is not a violent concept.*

- *Jihad is not a declaration of war against other religions. It is worth noting that the Koran specifically refers to Jews and Christians as "people of the book" who should be protected and respected. All three faiths worship the same God. Allah is just the Arabic word for God, and is used by Christian Arabs as well as Muslims.*

- *Military action in the name of Islam has not been common in the history of Islam. Scholars says most calls for violent jihad are not sanctioned by Islam.*

- *Warfare in the name of God is not unique to Islam. Other faiths throughout the world have waged wars with religious justifications.[3]*

Most inherently, at least for the enumerable dead and maimed (regardless of worldwide locale), it matters not a whit where its basic meaning, linguistically-speaking, is derived from. In any case, who cares, other than the actual perpetrators of militant jihad and those who seek to serve as their apologists and jive-talkers? But what does matter is its fiery end-result!

Inextricably, the barbaric handiwork of militant jihad can fill book after book, and with no end in sight. Nevertheless, certain stark illustrations must be placed front and center. One such gory (atypical) centerpiece took place on September 2, 2014 with the beheading of American journalist Steven Sotloff, in Syria.

Tuesday, September 2, the Islamist butchers of ISIS beheaded Steven Sotloff, a captured American journalist. Sotloff, who was kidnapped last year in Syria, was forced to read a statement condemning America, and then his throat was slowly cut with a hunting knife until his head was removed from his body. Of course, apologists for Islam will shout to the heavens that ISIS does not represent Islam, but it is becoming harder.

President Obama would have us believe Islam is truly the Religion of Peace. He condemned ISIS as completely un-Islamic when he spoke about their beheading of American journalist James Foley, before returning to the golf course to complete his round.

"So ISIL speaks for no religion. Their victims are overwhelmingly Muslim, and no faith teaches people to massacre innocents. No just God would stand for what they did yesterday, and for what they do every single day. ISIL has no ideology of any value to human beings. Their ideology is bankrupt. They may claim out of expediency that they are at war with the United States or the West, but the fact is they terrorize their neighbors and offer them nothing but an endless slavery to their empty vision, and the collapse of any definition of civilized behavior."

Yet Obama, who openly declares his love for the Quran after studying Islam since his childhood, certainly should know Islam's Holy Book actually encourages the behavior of ISIS. Quran (8:12) - "I will cast terror into the hearts of those who disbelieve. Therefore strike off their heads and strike off every fingertip of them". The viewpoint of ISIS echoes throughout the Islamic world. Mawlana Abul Ala Mawdudi, founder of Pakistan's Islamic Fundamentalist Movement, which boasts hundreds of thousands of members, spoke openly and honestly about the religion of Islam.

"Islam is a revolutionary faith that comes to destroy any government made by man. Islam doesn't look for a nation to be in better condition than another nation. Islam doesn't care about the land or who own the land. The goal of Islam is to rule the entire world and submit all of mankind to the faith of Islam. Any nation or power in this world that tries to get in the way of that goal, Islam will fight and destroy." [4]

Consequently, it must be internalized that Steven Sotlofff's ISIS captors adhered to the absolute Qur'anic-based concepts of jihad which are practiced throughout the Islamic world. For the record, Saudi Arabia, the erstwhile *partner* of many US administrations, is a *leader* in this field with upwards of 175 beheaded in 2015!

Saudi Arabia has executed at least 175 people in the past year, at a rate of one every two days, according to a report by Amnesty International.

The kingdom killed 102 convicted criminals in the first six months of 2015 alone, putting it on course to beat its 1995 record number for the calendar year of 192. Those killed included children under the age of 18 at the time of the offence, and disabled people.

Amnesty, which alongside the AFP news agency keeps a record of the number of people the Saudi government kills, said the execution rate suddenly surged in August last year and continued to rise under the new King Salman from January.

According to a new 44-page report released by the charity today, at least 2,208 people have been executed in Saudi Arabia since January 1985. [5]

Moving right along to the aforementioned working definition of jihad, yes, the above (and what follows) is not only factually correct, but where the truth lies. In no uncertain terms, western apologists

- those who insist upon explaining away Shariah-based barbarism by continuously harping on its *peaceful* nature - are as guilty as those who inflict the physical blows. Inestimably, they lend them *legitimate* PC cover and serve as their fig leaves for every heinous act imaginable. It's as simple as that.

Still yet, relative to its knock-on effects to the west, it is not enough to depend upon (in your mind's eye) all the ghoulish aspects of Islamic terrorism to set the record straight. In other words, a working knowledge base of the underpinnings of Islam is key and core, without which all context and texture is lost.

To that end, let us start with what is known as *stealth* jihad, aka civilization jihad. Accordingly, the key Muslim Brotherhood memo unearthed on this subject reveals:

> *In July 2007, seven key leaders of an Islamic charity known as the Holy Land Foundation for Relief and Development (HLF) went on trial for charges that they had: (a) provided 'material support and resources' to a foreign terrorist organization (namely Hamas); (b) engaged in money laundering; and (c) breached the International Emergency Economic Powers Act, which prohibits transactions that threaten American national security. Along with the seven named defendants, the U.S. government released a list of approximately three hundred "unindicted co-conspirators" and "joint venturers." During the course of the HLF trial, many incriminating documents were entered into evidence. Perhaps the most significant of these was "An Explanatory Memorandum on the General Strategic Goal for the Group in North America," by the Muslim Brotherhood operative Mohamed Akram. Federal investigators found Akram's memo in the home of Ismael Elbarasse, a founder of the Dar Al-Hijrah mosque in Falls Church, Virginia, during a 2004 search. Elbarasse was a member of the Palestine Committee, which the Muslim Brotherhood had created to support Hamas in the United States.*

Written some time in 1987 but not formally published until May 22, 1991, Akram's eighteen-page document listed the Brotherhood's twenty-nine likeminded "organizations of our friends" that shared the common goal of dismantling American institutions and turning the U.S. into a Muslim nation. These "friends" were identified by Akram and the Brotherhood as groups that could help convince Muslims "that their work in America is a kind of grand Jihad in eliminating and destroying the Western civilization from within and 'sabotaging' its miserable house by their hands . . . so that . . . God's religion [Islam] is made victorious over all other religions".[6]

Once the above is digested and taken to heart, attesting to their step-by-step planned takeover of America, which is the most important conquest in the Brotherhood's global ambitions, the next lesson learned comes from (none other than) Professor Paul Eidelberg. It is not for nothing that one of the co-authors of this book credited him in the acknowledgments.

Incontestably, the most incisive policy paper relative to militant jihad, "Islam and Blood" (July 2012), is attributed to this valiant professor and patriot. For full disclosure, I, Adina Kutnicki, had a hand in its review, was asked to contribute any thoughts and suggestions, and was deeply humbled. Be that as it may, its introduction sets the stage for a full scholarly rendition of the ineluctable aspects of Islam; political, cultural, and theological. Essays by well-respected individuals, mainly former Muslims who renounced their faith, apostates, are contained within its pages. The following serves as its introduction:

"America's Deadliest Enemy" by Professor Paul Eidelberg

That Muslims have exceeded the depravity of Nazis by using their own children as human bombs tends to hinder objective and comprehensive analysis of Islam. This essay will instead provide a thoroughly documented, interdisciplinary, transnational, and multiracial study of Islam which men with eyes and ears and a modicum of learning will discern as a unique form of paganism, one that sanctifies evil in the name of a monotheistic theology.

Prologue

It is well known that Islam today is a cauldron of murderous hatred. We are no longer shocked by the fact that Muslims hate not only non-Muslims but other Muslims. It is common knowledge that Sunnis and Shiites hate each other, that both abhor Sufi Muslims as well as other Islamic sects. True, something comparable to this may also be said of certain Christian sects before the Reformation—and we dare not forget that Christians slaughtered Jews down through the centuries. But as Dr. Michael Ledeen has documented, and as will presently be seen, Islam is unique in that its love of death or necrophilia remains an ineluctable aspect of its theology.

Moreover, despite the murderous hatred Muslim sects display toward each other, we need to understand the character of their supreme role-model and prophet, Mohammad, the author of their holy Scripture, the Quran.[2] We need to transcend vacuous tolerance, and we dare not yield to the timidity that poses as "moderation" in discussing Islam. We deplore the fact that Islam's cult of hatred and love of death is downplayed by scholars who are reluctant or incapable of revealing the theological underpinning of this hatred magnified by necrophelia. Indeed, scholars in the West are reluctant to say anything pejorative of a creed that poses as a worldwide monotheistic religion. We can no longer afford this reticence because weapons of mass murder are now available to this enemy. Our survival requires us to expose the ugly truths about this enemy. We need to understand why Muslims, whether they are Arabs in Saudi Arabia or Persians in Iran, hate Americans and Jews as well as each other. This is a fearful amount of hatred animating a strategically significant percentage of the estimated 1.5 billion Muslims on planet earth!

Is it not awesome that so many people who worship Allah can harbor so much hatred—enough to commit even genocide? This horrendous phenomenon is a terrible reflection on what civilized people deem a monotheistic religion. To clarify this theological mystery in a candid and convincing manner is precisely the primary concern of this essay. But first, we must come down to earth and remove the many obstacles that hinder this intellectually complex study of Islam without being deterred by its emotionally-charged consequences, which seem to silence polite commentators.

If Islam is indeed a cauldron of hatred that animates the leaders of 1.5 billion Muslims and dozens of Muslim states, is it any wonder that many people in the West see this awesome, widespread hostility as an irremediable and impossible threat? Is it any wonder that very few Western scholars and statesmen display the candor and courage to discuss the theological nature of this threat? What irony! The threat is from an enemy that defines us as the enemy—even though we sincerely profess to be truly benevolent and peace loving. Our benevolence is obvious. We are even reluctant to call our enemy an "enemy," let alone as our sworn and implacable enemy, lest we insinuate that this strange enemy is evil. We hesitate to use any pejorative language to describe this enemy, not only because we fear it may antagonize him and prompt him to violence, but also because we live in a non-judgmental age that avoids calling even an openly declared enemy evil—even one who gleefully screams "Death 2 to America" and vows to "wipe Israel off the map"! Some observers believe that the liberal and social democracies of the West are suffering from a mental disorder. Let me try to explain.

Whether conscious of it or not, people in the West have been subtly and profoundly influenced by the moral and cultural relativism that has permeated all levels of education in the free world. For more than a hundred years we have been indoctrinated by the ethical neutrality or indifferentism of the social sciences and humanities. Our institutions of higher education have taught countless opinion makers and policy makers that there are no rational or objective standards by which to distinguish between right and wrong, good or bad, and this inhibits us from calling any moral or religious doctrine pernicious. Describing any doctrine as evil is equivalent to calling someone's preference for a particular flavor of ice cream evil. It's all a matter of personal taste—nothing to get upset about, let alone to resort to violence.

And so it is with religion. Your religious preference has no more validity than your preference for light- or dark-rimmed glasses. The conflicts people wage over this or that religion or ideology is irrational. If everyone understood that there are no objective moral or religious truths, hence, that no way of life is intrinsically superior to any other, war would be a thing of the past. Tolerance and peace would rein on earth.

This naive relativism ignores a crucial fact: some men like to lord it over others, regardless of whether they are believers, agnostics, or atheists. But what is more: given two antagonists—one a moral relativist, the other a moral absolutist, then, all other things being equal, the absolutist is more likely to persevere and win in any protracted conflict. It is doubtful that the Allied Powers in the Second World War would have conquered Nazi Germany had they not believed that Nazism is evil, and that freedom or liberal democracy is worth fighting and dying for.

This is precisely the psychological state of affairs underlying or affecting the conflict between Islam and the United States— and this conflict began before 9/11. Muslims believe in the absolute righteousness of their cause, the cause of Islam, and that liberal democracy is evil. This moral disparity or asymmetry is precisely why the more powerful United States, whose decision-makers have been influenced and emasculated by multicultural relativism, is retreating from the Middle East, just as it retreated from Communist-led North Vietnam, a tenth-rate military power. But mark this well: as in the 1960s, American colleges and universities are not only steeped in multicultural relativism, as I have shown in an essay published in the Congressional Record,³ but we now behold academics professing outright anti-Americanism!

What does this portend? The bellicosity of the enemy is transparent. He harbors a 1,400 year-old military heritage. His mentality is permeated and disciplined by this heritage. His Arab-Islamic mind abhors infidels, and he is not reluctant to use weapons of mass murder. It should be obvious that the growing power of Iran in the oil-rich Persian Gulf and the expansion of the Muslim Brotherhood on the one hand, and America's retreat from the Middle East on the other, indicate that our enemy is winning in what can only be called a World War. What is most remarkable, however, is that America, the world's only superpower, has yet to define the enemy!

It would be easy to do this if Islam was an atheistic and geographically-defined regime like Nazi Germany or Communist Russia. But our enemy poses as a worldwide monotheistic religion, and here is where Islam departs from other cultures that exalt war. Islam, which should be credited for having eliminated idolatry in Asia and Africa, is a religion whose prophet forms an integral part of the faith. As I have elsewhere written, it is not sufficient to believe in the Scriptures of such prophets or messengers but in the messengers themselves. This is another reason why Muslims have wielded the sword to spread the faith and to send "infidels" to eternal rest. Compare the militant religion of the Hindus, another numerous people. The Hindus worship Shiva, the god of destruction. Their sacred text, the Bhagavid Gita, exalts war. Rulers, who necessarily come from the warrior caste, are obliged to discipline their subjects to wage aggressive wars against neighboring states whenever feasible. As one writer says: "Peace emerges from India's literature and history either as stagnation, or as a time for plotting military action, or as a ruse of war meant to induce somnolence and moral disarmament in enemy ranks." [4] Add Buddhism. Although Buddhism arose in protest against the Hindu caste system, it did not alter the prevailing orientation toward war and peace. In Japan, Zen Buddhism combined with Shintoism to establish the martial tradition (innocuously portrayed in the theatrical West). Throughout Southeast Asia warfare has been accepted as the natural expression of the religious or political order. Much the same may be said of all of the regions of sub-Saharan Africa. [5] But it is in China that the science of war achieved perfection. The martial classics of China exhort rulers to make their people "delight in war" and to expand the frontiers of the state. "It is a misfortune for a prosperous country not to be at war; for in peacetime it will breed . . .the cultivation of goodness, filial piety and respect for elders, detraction of war and shame at taking part in it." [6]

But we were talking of Islam, which, unlike those just mentioned, is deemed a monotheistic religion. And even though many of us are not religious, we tend to believe that, withstanding the wars in which Christian monotheists engaged in the past, the participants in these wars were actually violating their sacred creeds or scriptures. In other words, we want to believe that religion—at least monotheism—is basically benevolent and peace loving; and that even though history manifests bloody examples to the contrary, we incline to the idea that these wars may be attributed—stated simply—to either (1) intellectual causes, (2) moral causes, or (3) systemic causes, meaning, the *international system of sovereign states. The first may involve the miscalculations of statesmen regarding the interests of their respective countries. The second may involve the lust for power and dominion. The third may involve, as indicated, the nation-state system itself, which tends to intensify and magnify international conflict. Unfortunately, these considerations are only tangential to the core issues of this essay. Our Prologue must therefore be supplemented by an Introduction that clarifies the intractable nature of Islam and why this enemy constitutes a mortal threat to Western civilization, hence, to the Judeo-Christian heritage, the heart of this civilization.*

Introduction

"To speak of Judaism, Christianity, and Islam as the "three Abrahamic faiths," the 'three religions of the Book,' or the three monotheisms, obscures rather than illuminates. These familiar tropes ought to be retired." [7] *—George P. Weigel Catholic Theologian*

Some readers, who have not examined the profound scholarship of Dr. Weigel, may attribute his above pronouncement to the bias of a Catholic theologian. But there are many scholars and scholar statesmen—including atheists—who have not only expressed doubts about the authenticity of Islamic monotheism, but who also deny that Islam can rightly be called a civilization! Indeed, such doubts about Islam can be found even among many former Muslims!

Here caution is necessary. To obtain an objective and transnational as well as insiders understanding of Islam, let us consider how world-renowned scholar-statesmen evaluated Islam before 1900 that is, before the emotional impact and horrors of jihadism, and why learned Muslims abhor Islam and regard it as cruel and tyrannical. We begin with the world renowned nineteenth century thinker Alexis de Tocqueville, author of the classic Democracy in America:

I studied the Quran a great deal. I came away from that study with the conviction that by and large there have been few religions in the world as deadly to men as that of Muhammad. So far as I can see, it is the principal cause of the decadence so visible today in the Muslim world and, though less absurd than the polytheism of old, its social and political tendencies are in my opinion more to be feared, and I therefore regard it as a form of decadence rather than a form of progress in relation to paganism itself.

Compare a statement appearing in the 1899 work of Winston Churchill The River War:

Moslems may show splendid qualities, but the influence of the religion paralyses the social development of those who follow it. No stronger retrograde force exists in the world. Far from being moribund, Mohammedanism is a militant and proselytizing faith. It has already spread throughout Central Africa, raising fearless warriors at every step; and were it not that Christianity is sheltered in the strong arms of science, the science against which it had vainly struggled, the civilization of modern Europe might fall, as fell the civilization of ancient Rome.[9]

Perhaps some may attribute the assessments of de Tocqueville and Churchill to imperialistic bias or even to racism. Indeed, in as much as criticism of Islam exposes one to the racist canard, let us ponder the views and experience of intellectually liberated Muslims and Arabs. Indeed, perhaps the most reliable way to assess the nature of Islam is to consult such commentators. For this purpose, we can do no better than examine the transnational evidence and records of personal experience contained in the website. [7]

It can be accessed, in its entirety, at the following link: https://adinakutnicki.files.wordpress.com/2012/07/islam_and_blood.pdf.

Along these same historical lines, Thomas Jefferson, in dealing with the Barbary pirates, Muslim kingdoms engaged in piracy and kidnapping on the high seas, read the Qur'an to see if it was possible to negotiate with them. Finding no common ground, he dispatched the Navy and Marine Corps to deal with them. Hence, America's first foreign conflict and the source of the line in the "Marine Corps Hymn," "to the shores of Tripoli."[8]

Inherently, have Americans forgotten their history to the degree that too many are incapable of drawing the salient parallels between militant jihad of yesteryear and that of today, that which really are one and the same? Most significantly, above all else, it will be through a non-sanitized version of the underlying political, cultural and quasi-religious basis of Islam that western civilization will be saved. Rest assured, without the proper lessons learned, as always, it is verily impossible to fight back. It's a bit like chasing ghosts.

In light of the above, the following (which was reported on by one of the co-authors, and re-blogged at several highly-trafficked sites) is more than noteworthy to internalize because it involves a major hub of militant jihadists (ISIS plays a central part) operating and stirring deep inside the heart of Massachusetts. Learn said lessons well. Still yet, beforehand, bear upmost in mind that this is the same jacked-up Muslim Brotherhood jihadi arena which witnessed the blow up of Boston's Marathon on April 15, 2013. It is a veritable cesspool of activity.

http://www.history.com/this-day-in-history/three-people-killed-hundreds-injured-in-boston-marathon-bombing

In this regard, readers should hardly be shocked that a particular plot is brewing right under the "watchful" eyes and ears of the federal government. Alas, they are unperturbed, nonplussed. Wait and see. In brief, the following exposé is duly instructive:

It has come to this investigative journalist's attention that an ongoing and major money laundering operation – For the benefit of Sunni jihadi terror – is housed in a town (its exact name is being held in abeyance, at least for now) within Barnstable County, and with an offshoot in Hyannis, the largest of its seven villages . . .

The "persons of interest", living in Massachusetts, are Sunni Muslims from a very large clan spread throughout Lebanon. While this part of the Middle East is mostly well known for its Shia/Hezbollah/Tehran axis – over 54 percent of Lebanese are Muslim – approximately 27 percent are Sunni. [10]

It is into this spider's web that money/gold laundering comes into play. So, what's the upshot?

An entire clan operates as successful jewelry entrepreneurs, owning upwards of fifty stores which are "related" to this particular type of militant jihad operation. Even more so, they have a distinct presence within community-based organizations and clubs, similar to many successful retailers. In essence, they are hiding in plain sight.

Moreover, they also own several homes in the same general vicinity. Basically, they are deeply involved in buying a lot of stolen gold with cash from their aforementioned businesses. In the main, retail businesses (in the hands of white collar criminals or terror-related financing launderers) can accumulate stashes of unreported cash for this and that. One oft-utilized mechanism is through the under-reporting of sales, whereby receipts barely reflect the actual income generated.

Thus, sales tax and other mandatory taxes are negligible, ipso facto; hordes of cash can be stowed away. As to the "possibilities," use your imagination.

Moving right along, once the gold is horded it has to be melted into proper form. As a result, the clan uses one of their homes as a central melting base, the end product being gold bars approximately 10×1 in size. How very entrepreneur-like.

Now, what's their next phase to said operation? Well, the gold must be moved out of the country and back into Lebanon, and this requires a certain level of "cooperation" from other contacts. In any case, the gold bars are secreted within special luggage compartments, to be hauled back by visiting family members – mostly via "tourist" visas – who act as mules upon returning to Lebanon. Understood?

Not only that, but some of their cash wends its way through the purchase of additional hard assets. Pointedly, a willing home owner received a substantial sum of cash – without having to report said sale to the IRS – and these monies became laundered through a new home. A win-win on both ends. Nevertheless, for the purposes of this discussion, the "subjects of interest" utilize various layers to fund jihad. Enough said.

Regardless, once the gold bars reach Lebanon they require a reliable address for laundering. Essentially, a very specific (Middle Eastern- based and operated) financial investment firm acts as their main monetary slush house. Lebanon is one of their hubs.

Now, which group receives an abundance of cash from their laundered money/gold? Well, the HABBASH Group is a main recipient and it is a branch of al-Qaeda in Lebanon! Recall this tidbit: ISIS is an offshoot of al-Qaeda, its forerunner!

Most significantly, an informant (vetted by Dave Gaubatz, an impeccably credentialed counterterrorism contact) handed over very detailed information (which is not posted for various security reasons) with names, addresses, travel plans, etc., to relevant federal agencies.

These agencies included the FBI, the Attorney General's Office in Massachusetts and the IRS. They all refused to investigate said charges. Why? How can this be?

Conclusively, the following response to said (courageous) informant should serve as prima facie evidence (Exhibit One), attesting to the FEDS utter refusal to even look into the charges, which more than met the criteria for immediate investigation. . . [9]

Along this alleged gold/money laundering trail, as far back as 2011, the aforementioned vetted informant first made contact with the Attorney General's Office in Massachusetts. Basically, he dropped in their laps a militant Islamic jihad related road map to the "follow the gold/money" operation. However, as the following emails (a sampling of the correspondence can be found below, while others are held back for various reasons) provided by Gaubatz and reprinted with permission will demonstrate, the Feds declined. Simply put, they weren't all that interested in following the droppings already gifted, nor to find out "what else was in the informant's bag."

XXXX to Mr. Downing, July 28, 2011:

Dear Mr Downing,

I would like to report a money laudering business done by the AKKAWI family.

Let me tell first about this family:

- 4 brothers (Mustapha, Saleh, Mohamed & Fadi)who own 2 franchises Hannoush jewelers one in Falmouth & the other one in Hyannis.

- They are Sunni muslim & members of the HABBASH group in Lebanon.It's an extremist group like the WAHABE where osama bin laden belonged. It is a branch of alquaida in Lebanon. They give a lot of money to that group.

Now about the money laudering. Using Hannoush jewelers they buy a lot of stolen gold with cash after that they melt the gold into long bars approx 10 by 1 " & after that they put those bars in their luggages & travel to Lebanon. Now their mother & kids are visiting US & they will use them as mules to transport the gold to Lebanon.

The gold melting is done in East Falmouth in one of their 3 houses.

You need to do your own investigating.

I will let you know when they leaving the US to go back.

Another money laudering happened last year when mustapha akkawi bought a building from one of his employee her name is XXXX who lives @ XXXX Mashpee Ma, He gave her $250,000 in CASH got a loan 0f $250,000 with a partner named XXXX , now XXXX never declared the $250,000 in cash & didn't have to pay any taxes, and Mustapha got rid of the $250,000 in cash & didn't pay any taxes. Where the $250,000 came? From the 2 jewelry stores where a lot of cash transactions were done NO RECEIPTS NO TAXES.

I have more in my bag to say.

Sincerely,

XXXX

And while the only response from the AG's office was a mix between boilerplate, coupled with there is no "there, there" - despite enough actionable intelligence to choke a horse - undeterred, in the interim, the investigation continued.

In 2015, Gaubatz reached out to the Massachusetts Attorney General (he contacted the FBI in the first quarter of 2016), as well as to various media outlets, wondering, why no investigation ensued, even though very specific gold/money laundering evidence was provided.

Dave Gaubatz to XXXX, Brad Stone, Eric Shawn, March 19, 2015:

For Ms. Martha Coakly (State Attorney General MA), Recently a Mr. XXXXXX who is originally from Lebanon and now lives in your area provided you very detailed information about current Islamic terrorist activity in the Boston area. Your Criminal Division refused to act on very, very detailed evidence about serious Jihadist activity. Why?

Millions of people now want to know. A media source from Israel wrote an extensive article today about the Jihadist activity in your area and how your office, the IRS, and the FBI refused to listen to a man who had extensive details with names, businesses, and others about CURRENT Jihadist activity in Boston.

Your office and the other agencies have been very negligent in protecting the people in MA. I would like to interview you about this case. XXXX and I have talked several times and all I could do was shake my head when I heard State and Federal authorities ignored him. I was a U.S. Federal Agent for over 15 years and the ignoring of current Jihadist activity is not only a bad decision, but likely a criminal offense.

If citizens have detailed information about Jihadist activity, it is my opinion the information should be taken seriously. I think the people of Boston would like to know why the MA State Attorney General, the IRS, and the FBI, are not protecting the people and our country.

http://adinakutnicki.com/2015/05/08/islamic-moneygold-laundering-in-massachusetts-finances-jihadfeds-ignore-evidence-what-can-be-done-commentary-by-adina-kutnicki/

Respectfully,

Dave Gaubatz
U.S. Federal Agent (retired)
Author: 'Muslim Mafia'
www.wearenotafraid.blogspot.com

For the record, it was not unusual for Gaubatz to reach out to this co-author for her "assistance" in various ways, as repeatedly hinted at below.

Dave Gaubatz to XXXX, March 8, 2015:

The suspects are Muslims in Boston. Two sleeper cells. They buy stolen gold and send to terror groups such as ISIS. They make around 1 million a month to send to terrorists. They own jewelry stores in Boston. The source knows all the details.

Dave Sent from my iPhone

Consequently, another "shout out" became necessary when things heated up - despite the lack of "interest" by the FEDS!

Dave Gaubatz to XXXX, Mar 29, 2015

The source went to the Feds with names, businesses, and the who, what, when, where, and how. They made him feel like crap and would not answer his calls. I see this happening all over. Muslims are being recruited as FBI Agents, at the State Department and White House. We will press on. I will put together a straight forward report for you.

Dave g Sent from my iPhone

(Un)holy jihad....

As such, let us raptly turn our attention to the piggybacked danger that is social media. This book will conclusively prove that it dovetails, props up, and otherwise lends cover to militant jihad. Furthermore, let it be known: Social media is the leading purveyor and incubator for deadly exchanges between Allah's soldiers across the globe, and this is aside from the plots devised within mosques worldwide. Indeed, it affords them a virtual and communal home to meet, greet, and to otherwise share *recipes*. In turn, this ratchets up their ability to give *moral* and material support to one another. Intrinsically, they are gifted the freedom to plot, in what amounts to the slaughtering of as many infidels as possible. No doubt, the number one platform which serves as their helpmate is Facebook. It is a fiefdom unto itself. Resultant, its knock-on effects are such that western civilization, as we know it, has the potential to be altered for *time immemorial*.

CHAPTER THREE

WHAT DOES THE OBAMA ADMINISTRATION, THE "FOURTH ESTATE," AND ACADEMIA HAVE IN COMMON?

I t is hardly accidental, nor incidental, that alternative media exploded onto the scene when it did. It is mainly, but not exclusively, web-based. This medium catapulted into the spotlight in the mid-1990's and has been, blessedly, going at full-force steam ever since. Even though over two decades old, it is, historically speaking, still in its infancy.

> *Online news websites began to proliferate in the 1990s. An early adopter was* The News Observer *in Raleigh, North Carolina which offered online news as Nando. Steve Yelvington wrote on the Poynter Institute website about Nando, owned by The N&O, by saying "Nando evolved into the first serious, professional news site on the World Wide Web". It originated in the early 1990s as "NandO Land". It is believed that a major increase in digital online journalism occurred around this time when the first commercial web browsers, Netscape Navigator (1994), and Internet Explorer (1995). By 1996, most news outlets had an online presence.* [1]

First and foremost, conservative journalists and thinkers understood – well before most – that their voices were being continuously muted and stifled, if not outright distorted, within the "go to" mega media outlets. In this regard, it became imperative to seek out alternative forums for their reporting and analysis. Hence, the absolute gravitation and attraction towards digital media began.

That being said, the web was equally attractive for left-based outlets, but for wholly divergent reasons. In the main, it was increasingly obvious that a preponderance of readers were utilizing web-based platforms to glean the news of the day. Thereby, to maintain their edge and grip, as well as their financial bottom line, the calculus was abundantly clear: Jump on board! However, like sore losers are wont to do, once conservatives gained a larger megaphone through the web, suddenly, the Democrats (in lockstep with the aforementioned mega media outlets, and Republican In Name Only counterparts) decided that new regulations on the internet must be imposed! Hence, the Federal Elections Commission (FEC) was called into action, thus, to *regulate* political content and speech on the internet. Credo quia absurdum.[2]

Even so, a historical perspective is in order, if only to internalize how the once *even-handed* outlets morphed from there to here. In other words, how they became co-opted and captured entities.

In a nutshell, out of what used to be sixty companies, the media, since 1983, is now owned – lock, stock and barrel – by six mega corporations. They include: News Corp, Disney, Viacom, Time Warner, the Columbia Broadcasting System, and Comcast. Effectively, while it may appear that readers have a choice to view the news of the day, well, it is little more than a magician's sleight of hand. Illusory.

How did this happen? While a myriad of confluent forces precipitated said media takeover, two stand at the helm: While Federal Communications Commission deregulation started the process, the imposition of leftist group-think messaging within America's campuses became central players and components. In particular, its schools of journalism pushed the collusive media process forward. As to the first corrosive link:

Mark S. Fowler once observed, television is really nothing more than "a toaster with pictures."

Therein lay the essential philosophy on broadcasting that was the bedrock of Mr. Fowler's five-year reign as chairman of the five-member Federal Communications Commission. Mr. Fowler sought to demystify broadcasting, to remove it from the guarded realm of public trust to the freewheeling marketplace of private commerce.

Mr. Fowler, who is 45-years-old, said Friday that he would leave the F.C.C. in the spring. His program of deregulation has brought radical change to the industry, ranging from network takeovers to the rise of home shopping networks.

In the Fowler era, broadcasting licenses, once rigorously monitored by the F.C.C., became commodities traded on the open market. Stations changed hands overnight and then changed hands again in a flurry of speculation, profit-taking and -inevitably- miscalculation and bankruptcy. The public interest, Mr. Fowler said, would be determined by the "public's interest." That is, if the public didn't like the way a broadcaster was running a station, the enterprise would fail; the public didn't need the Government's help, "An Electronic Midway".

But critics of deregulation saw Mr. Fowler's vision as an abdication of the commission's responsibility for the public airwaves. They have blamed deregulation for a lowering of standards in programming, the de-stabilization of the networks, an increased permissiveness on television and the jeopardizing of children's and public affairs programming.

"What we see on the air now," said Fred W. Friendly, a former president of CBS News and now a professor at the Columbia Graduate School of Journalism, "is an electronic midway." Mr. Friendly and other critics have said deregulation has

replaced broadcasters with investors, businessmen interested in maximizing profits rather than serving the public "interest, convenience, and necessity" - the mandate articulated in the Communications Act of 1934.

Probably the most far-reaching change made by the Fowler commission was its decision early in the Reagan administration to rescind the F.C.C.'s anti-trafficking regulation, which stated that a broadcaster had to operate a station for three years before selling the license. "You could make a case that that was the single biggest thing that has happened in broadcasting in modern history,"" said the senior vice president of the CBS Broadcast Group, David Fuchs, in a telephone interview. "It's had a colossal effect. It's the reason for Capital Cities merging with ABC, it's the reason for Ted Turner trying to buy CBS, it's the reason for NBC being acquired."[3]

More specifically, a battle of sorts, a tug of war between old and new media is playing out at *The New Republic*, a century-old far left magazine. A venerable institution, if you will.

On the one hand, its storied history is steeped in the culture of so-called old media, coupled with the fact that it was never meant to be a money making venture, per se. Rather, over the years, its value has always been within its niche, resonating as the voice and barometer of the far left. In this regard, benefactors propped up its financial bottom line, so to speak.

But that was then and this is now. Ever since Facebook co-founder Chris Hughes bought up the cash-strapped entity (likely, presenting an offer they couldn't refuse) less than four years ago, revolt after revolt roiled within the magazine's key staff. As such, many have jumped ship.

Essentially, there are certain *rules* within institutionalized old media that are inviolate, and clearly Chris Hughes failed to learn this lesson.[4] Consequentially, as a knock-on effect, deregulation manifested into opportunities for a preponderance of US academics, most of whom tilt to the left. Truth dare be told, many of their careers are wedded to the "Fourth Estate." Resultant, increasingly restless and emboldened left-leaning academics jumped into what became a free-for-all media mentality. Nevertheless, this *marriage* didn't occur overnight. In reality, the courtship is decades old. It is both wholly unprofessional and morally bankrupt for professors to be injecting their political biases into their classrooms and campuses.

Basically, the 1960's afforded a hyper-organized group of well-funded student revolutionaries their foothold to overturn academia. Their efforts piggybacked onto an American landscape which was already on fire from various trigger points. Thus, they pounced into action across campuses, as well as throughout the national landscape. However, it must be understood that even though a cadre of student leaders were up to their necks in upending the social order by acting as campus foot soldiers, nevertheless, without the imprimatur, overt or covert, of faculties and administrators, the mayhem would not have been allowed to continue apace.

That being said, though several campuses were instigators and leaders in all the mayhem, Columbia University in New York City, most notably, *deserves* much of the credit. Starting in 1967-1968, the campus roiled with violent protests, so much so that buildings were overtaken by radicals and their behind the scenes supporters. Ostensibly, their pretext was having found out that the institutional apparatus supported the United States Government in the Vietnam War, but that was (mostly) a smokescreen.

Be that as it may, the die was cast. And it was into this nightmarish upheaval that leftist entrenchment into academia became cemented. Consequentially, so-called journalists are plucked from top journalism programs to fill *rarefied* openings at various media outlets. Of course, the most coveted ones are those within the *big six outlets*. One such prestigious program is Columbia School of Journalism, therefore, is it any wonder that alternative media became the only antidote to the "Fourth Estate"?

Most perniciously, these same yesteryear revolutionary student *activists* were groomed to take over academia's leadership from their predecessors who *tolerated* the overturning of the campuses to begin with – and takeover they did!

How many recall two domestic terror groups, the Weathermen and the Black Panthers? If not, time to catch up to speed. For the record, the Black Panthers are still going strong, albeit, under a re-branding, a *koshering* of sorts: The *New* Black Panthers! Mind you, they are part and parcel of Black Lives Matter.

In a related intersection, in April 2013, one of the co-authors was asked to pen a review for the reintroduction (originally published in1976) of *Bringing Down America: An FBI Informant with the Weathermen*, by Larry Grathwohl and Frank Reagan. Its basis is not only wholly germane to the topic at hand, but should be considered prima facie evidence of the same.

During a dangerously volatile period of domestic terrorism, young anarchists were plotting the upending of America. In the vanguard stood the Weather Underground and the Black Panthers. Implanted in 1969 in the heart of a revolutionary movement, Larry Grathwohl, a 22-year-old Vietnam vet, found himself acting as an FBI informant. Inserted into the Weather Underground organization under deep cover, he became privy to their terror plots as well as the leadership's "reasoning". It is this facet which still resonates today. BRINGING DOWN AMERICA is a gripping tale of plots and subplots, each one aimed at "the violent overthrow of the bourgeoisie [and] the establishment of the dictatorship of the proletariat", as Bill Ayers, Bernadine Dohrn, and Jeff Jones exhorted in their 1974 manifesto, "Prairie Fire: The Politics of Revolutionary Anti-Imperialism.""" The subtext of this gripping memoir is brought to the fore in Chapter 14: "The Cover Is Blown:"

"Once in the van we drove around the city . . .while we were driving Maynard & Green (my FBI handlers) began telling

me about the mystery man waiting for me. He was an Arab guerrilla. My meeting was to be in strict confidence. They refused to tell me why he was in the country, how he got in, obviously he was working for the U.S. . . ."

The implication was very clear. The FBI understood that the Weathermen were deepening their foreign ties. It was inevitable that Arab terror contacts would be made. Thus, Ali Baba, an Arab informant, was sending a warning to Larry: having him as a "go-between" would mitigate any hesitation to cooperate with the Weathermen, in effect, keeping the FBI one step ahead.

Not only that, Ali Baba issued other warnings to Larry: "the Arabs plan to strike at the next Olympic games in 1972 [reviewer's note: and they made good on their threat] and there is talk of doing something at the World's Fair in Spokane in 1974."

For the record, El (Al) Fatah was the referenced Arab guerrilla group. Yes, the very same terror outfit spawned by the godfather of suicide terror, "Chairman" Yasir Arafat, a recipient of the Nobel Peace Prize. In tandem, the Weathermen conspired with the KGB and attendant communist regimes. The war being waged against the U.S. by the radical left and Islamist jihadis is premised on the U.S. as the Western spear and Israel as its twin "imperialistic" cousin. It has been playing out for decades, in one form or another. Nothing has changed other than the fact that many escaped justice and are entering their senior years. Despite their advancing age, they are as dangerous as ever -- perhaps more so. Bill Ayers, the foremost leader of the Weathermen "is in his third decade as a national leader in the movement to radicalize the educational training of schoolteachers". His wife, Bernardine Dohrn, a top leader too "is a professor of law at Northwestern and a high-ranking officer in the American Bar Association." Eleanor Raskin (ne Stein) "is a law professor at S.U.N.Y Albany and, astonishingly, a NYS administrative law judge". Jeff Jones "currently heads the New York-based Apollo Alliance, a highly influential coalition of labor leaders and environmentalists, and was responsible for drafting President Obama's 2009 Recovery Act."

The list of "respectable" cover, of other "notables" in the Weathermen, is equally impressive. Through a stringently planned operational "stealth jihad", yesteryear's Weathermen have returned, fully primed to carry out their original goal -- the "transformation" of America. Most significantly, they subvert the national interest from a distinctly dangerous vantage point. They are currently ensconced in some of the most powerful positions in academia and political life. The only difference is, this time they are dressed in "capitalist" garb, not only in their clothing choices, but in the wealth they have accumulated, paradoxically, through joining the "establishment". Who said one can't enrich oneself, but at the same time deny the masses/proletariat said wealth potential? Highly dangerous in their bomb-making days, their capacity to cripple America, sans firing actual weaponry is that much greater at this critical juncture in time. Deeply involved in the "transformation" process, as promised by President Obama, many of them working inside the executive branch, while others operate through progressive think tanks, they want nothing more than to distance themselves from their bloody past. Therefore, an omertà has descended from the denizens of the leftist media and their powerful organs.[5]

More specifically, while an entire book can be written about the subversive nature of the Obama administration and the dangers accrued due to their domestic and foreign wildfires, it is their empowerment of militant Islamist jihadists, Sunni and Shia alike, which will eventually bring down America and the entire west. It is for this reason that one of the co-authors of this book was asked to offer her expertise via a comprehensive policy paper, which was commissioned to alert the public as to the whys and wherefores, regarding the administration's uncompromising quest to empower Iran as a nuclear-armed (rogue) state.

Thus, the "House of Bribes," by USATransnationalReport.org, was born. Its thoroughly documented basis leaves no doubt as to the sinister collusion, the marriage, between the Obama administration and Iran's genocidal mullahs. Inherently, its Executive Summary and Preface are excerpted below. The rest of the report delineates the ultimate western betrayal.

Executive Summary

The Iranian nuclear deal is a full capitulation to Iran's terrorist mastermind Mullahs, and the latest in a series of betrayals of the American people and allies by the Obama administration. At the highest level of the administration, Barack Obama's Senior Advisor, the Iranian-born Valerie Jarrett, prioritized rapprochement with the terror state. Throughout the process and negotiations, she had the backing of billionaire investor (and Obama-backer) George Soros, and his multi-headed network of tax-exempt foundations. Their efforts were driven by deep-rooted anti-Semitism and personal greed. Meanwhile, since the mid-1990s, a small but very connected Iranian lobby (funded, in part, by George Soros) has been laying the groundwork for normalizing relations with Tehran. Operating through a variety of non-governmental organizations and political action committees, the lobby courted Democrat and Republican politicians. With the election of (Soros-backed) Obama in 2008, the Iranian lobby had very receptive ears in the White House. International business interests were courted and effectively bribed with access to Iranian markets, until finally the deal was realized, approved, and sealed by a vote of the United Nations Security Council.

Preface

Thus far, the reports and exposés issued by the New Coalition of Concerned Citizens have focused on the threat posed by Islamists to American sovereignty. The Qatar Awareness Campaign brought to light extensive influence network of the State of Qatar and their ruling al-Thani family. The Betrayal Papers explained the Muslim Brotherhood's domination of the Obama administration's agenda and policies, foreign and domestic.

This report will detail the sinister influence of the small, yet well-connected and very powerful, Iran lobby. Though the Iran lobby's highest level contacts are prominent Democrats, their reach spans both major political parties. Like previous exposés, this investigation will mention familiar names, including George Soros, Valerie Jarrett, and the United Nations.

Iran is widely regarded by counterterrorism experts as the heart of Islamic radicalism, and the point of origin for terrorism with a specific geopolitical agenda (i.e., the creation of an Islamic Caliphate, much like the Islamic State, but dominated by Shiites, not Sunnis). With the eager embrace of a legacy-hungry Obama administration, the Iran lobby managed to achieve a deal which makes the United States the de facto most powerful backer of Islamic terrorism in the world.

How did this happen? . . .

House of Bribes: How the United States led the way to a Nuclear Iran is a product of: Adina Kutnicki, Andrea Shea King, Dr. Ashraf Ramelah, Benjamin Smith, Brent Parrish, Charles Ortel, Denise Simon, Dick Manasseri, Gary Kubiak, Hannah Szenes, Right Side News, Marcus Kohan, General Paul E. Vallely, Regina Thomson, Scott Smith, Terresa Monroe-Hamilton, Colonel Thomas Snodgrass, Trevor Loudon, Wallace Bruschweiler, and William Palumbo [6]

Stipulated, little is more collusive and corrosive, other than "journalist" spinmeisters who front for a wholly compromised and non-transparent administration. Talk about a force multiplier.

Even more so, Ben Rhodes, a high-level adviser to President Obama, brazenly and unabashedly admits to having the so-called mainstream media in the administration's pocket. So what else is left to say? Plenty.

Most significantly, a clear nexus exists between the Executive Branch and the "Fourth Estate" (again, schooled within leftist academia), which is less than six degrees separated. Incontrovertibly, the expectation should be nothing less than propaganda-like "journalism", spun a la like-minded ideologues.

For the record, Rhodes (his official title is "Assistant to the President and Deputy National Security Adviser for Strategic Communications and Speech writing"), President Obama's smug foreign policy adviser, audaciously admitted to using mainstream media to accomplish his goals.

Claims that some in the press are "in bed with the Obama Administration," are usually scoffed at by the mainstream media and progressive Democratic colleagues. In this piece, Rhodes repeatedly explains how he "ventriloquizes" the media, and he is happy about this accomplishment.

On the day Obama was to deliver his 2016 State of The Union Address, Iran captured and briefly held, U.S. Navy sailors. Rhodes told the Timeshow he managed the story by exploiting his "well-cultivated network of officials, talking heads, columnists and newspaper reporters." The Times reports:

Rhodes quickly does the political math on the breaking Iran story. "Now they'll show scary pictures of people praying to the supreme leader," he predicts, looking at the screen. Three beats more, and his brain has spun a story line to stanch the bleeding. He turns to Price [his deputy], "We're resolving this, because we have relationships," he says.

Price turns to his computer and begins tapping away at the administration's well-cultivated network of officials, talking heads, columnists and newspaper reporters, web jockeys and outside advocates who can tweet at critics and tweak their stories backed up by quotations from "senior White House officials" and "spokespeople." I watch the message bounce from Rhodes's brain to Price's keyboard to the three big briefing podiums — the White House, the State Department and the Pentagon — and across the Twitterverse, where it springs to life in dozens of insta-stories, which over the next five hours don formal dress for mainstream outlets. It's a tutorial in the making of a digital news microclimate — a storm that is easy to mistake these days for a fact of nature, but whose author is sitting next to me right now.

(. . .) The narratives he frames, the voices of senior officials, the columnists and reporters whose work he skillfully shapes and ventriloquizes, and even the president's own speeches and talking points, are the only dots of color in a much larger vision about who Americans are and where we are going that Rhodes and the president have been formulating together over the past seven years . . .[7]

But if anything smacks of catastrophic knock-on effects due to the Obama administration's misconduct, in cooperation with a lock-step media (of which Facebook is part and parcel), look no further than to a "skilled storyteller duping America into passing the Iran deal." By his own admission, the noxious and immorally-bent storyteller, Rhodes, intoned:

The Obama administration cooked up a phony story to sell Americans on the Iranian nuke deal, lying that US officials were dealing with "moderates" in the Islamic theocracy who could be trusted to keep their word, it was reported Thursday.

In a revealing article posted on the New York Times *website, President Obama's foreign-policy guru Ben Rhodes bragged about how he helped create the false narrative because the public would not have accepted the deal had it known that Iranian hard-liners were still calling the shots.*

The White House line — which Rhodes says he created — was that Obama started negotiations after the supposedly moderate Hassan Rouhani was elected president in 2013.

But Obama had set his sights on working out a deal with the mad mullahs as early as 2008, and negotiations actually began when strongman Mahmoud Ahmadinejad was still president.

Rhodes, the deputy national security adviser for strategic communications, concedes in the article that the so-called moderate regime is not moderate at all.

"We're not betting on it," he said.

Despite having little foreign-policy experience, Rhodes, 38, a former aspiring novelist who grew up on the Upper East Side, was in charge of a massive White House "messaging" effort that fed the bogus line to journalists.

"We created an echo chamber. They were saying things that validated what we had given them to say," he admitted in the Times interview when asked about the plethora of "experts" praising the deal in the press.

The Times article, which will appear in the paper's Sunday magazine, notes Rhodes, who has a writing degree from NYU, was skilled as a "storyteller."

"He is adept at constructing overarching plotlines with heroes and villains, their conflicts supported by flurries of carefully chosen adjectives, quotations and leaks from named and unnamed senior officials," reporter David Samuels writes. "He is the master shaper and retailer of Obama's foreign-policy narratives."

Asked about his misleading version of the deal, Rhodes said, "In the absence of rational discourse, we are going to discourse the [expletive] out of this". . . .[8]

Now that that is settled, effectively, the cat is out of the bag relative to the incestuous relationship between the Executive Branch and their media lapdogs.

Conclusively, that which took place in the 1960's and 1970's is roiling to this day to catastrophic ends. The above must be internalized as direct knock-on effects due to an *unholy trinity*; an absolute alliance between American (western) leadership, leftward based media, and their academic counterparts. Incontestably, the triad are in deep sympathy with militant jihad.

Said *unholy trinity* was given some exposure in mid-2016 when a former Facebook employee told Gizmodo that conservative news items and sites were routinely censored or blacklisted from the social media site's Trending Topics section.[9]

Worse yet, according to the reports, topics like Black Lives Matter were actually made to trend by Facebook employees who reportedly *injected* them so as to make them trend.

Facebook denied the reports, but the damage was done. In an effort to smooth over ruffled feathers, company leadership invited a hand-picked group of conservative *leaders* for a face-to-face meeting.

One of those in attendance, radio talk show host Glenn Beck, said he believed Zuckerberg was sincere because he looks people in the eye when he addresses them. Others, however, weren't so certain and said Beck spent the meeting essentially auditioning to be the Facebook CEO's *manservant*.

More indicting, John Thune, the senior Senator from South Dakota, had this to say: "Facebook must answer these serious allegations and hold those responsible to account if there has been political bias in the dissemination of trending news. "Any attempt by a neutral and inclusive social media platform to censor or manipulate political discussion is an abuse of trust and inconsistent with the values of an open Internet."[10]

Adding fuel to the accusations made by Facebook's courageous (Trending Topics section) whistleblower, along comes a World Net Daily Exclusive, and its headline is more than fiery: "Facebook Bias: It's Baked into the Algorithms." Now, them's fighting words.

But before a smattering of their evidence is presented, it is not lost on this co-author that the (higher) mathematical term, algorithm, is enough to cause some to swoon or roll their eyes. No shame in admitting that. Regardless, read on and learn.

WASHINGTON – A four-month WND study of Facebook traffic and engagement patterns of prominent alternative news sites with a more "conservative" perspective confirms recent charges that the social-media giant actually ignores its own rules and guidelines at the expense of these online enterprises.

The issue of Facebook bias erupted just recently when former staffers who worked on the company's Trending Topics fixture said in a report in the tech blog Gizmodo they were told to suppress certain conservative issues, and promote liberal topics.

The company explained that the Trending Topics stories are picked by a software formula, and then reviewed by staff members, and Facebook founder Mark Zuckerberg first denied the social network's editors suppress conservative news from its website feature.

Zuckerberg then went further, saying he wants to invite "leading conservatives and people from across the political spectrum" to talk about the allegations about "Trending Topics" on his website.

He said he couldn't find evidence to support the concerns.

Facebook Vice President of Search Tom Stocky went further, denying the allegations, writing on the site:

"My team is responsible for Trending Topics, and I want to address today's reports alleging that Facebook contractors manipulated Trending Topics to suppress stories of interest to conservatives. We take these reports extremely seriously, and have found no evidence that the anonymous allegations are true."

But statistics generated by Facebook itself may conflict with that determination.

And WND CEO Joseph Farah said a meeting is a good idea.

"If Zuckerberg wants to meet with someone whose business was victimized by his company, he just needs to tell me where the meeting is," he said.

WND used data provided by Facebook itself to page managers (Facebook.com/WNDNews) in its insights tab, and tracked several news sites through the Pages to Watch feature since the start of 2016.

The result uncovered was that, even though the number of "likes" on such sites has gone up, the rates of engagement have gone down.

Significantly.

WND compared the performance of the WND page posts and posts with similar pages on Facebook to track weekly growth and engagement versus the growth and engagement of competitors.

This offers insight on how WND, and other companies like TheBlaze.com, DailyCaller.com, Breitbart.com and IJReview. com are performing on Facebook through the metrics of Total Page Likes and the Engagement for the week the page had.

Facebook defines Engagement rate as the percentage of people who saw a post and reacted to, shared, clicked or commented on it. Factors that influence engagement rate include users' comments, shares and likes.

WND divided engagement by total page likes to get the engagement as percentage of fan base number. This was the manner WND tried to determine the value of increasing the total likes for a fan page. For competitive analysis, WND wanted to measure growth versus similar pages.

At the end of January 2016:

TheBlaze.com had 1.8 million likes and an engagement rate of 27.59 percent (of the total fan base)

Breitbart.com had 1.6 million likes and an engagement rate of 100 percent

WND.com had 568,000 likes and an engagement rate of 38.47 percent

DailyCaller.com had 1.4 million likes and an engagement rate of 41.58 percent

Washington Free Beacon had 621,300 likes and an engagement rate of 27.97 percent

Washington Examiner had 599,000 likes and an engagement rate of 43.29.

As of May 9, 2016, the drops in activity were significant in most cases.

As of that date, WND had compiled a sample-size of four months of data to showcase how engagement for those news sites had seen significant drops in engagement, seemingly supporting accusations by former Facebook employees of internal newsfeed tampering . . .[11]

And those who believe that only *knuckle-draggers* in America, you know, the incendiary term used by so-called liberals when speaking about conservatives, and that's when they are behaving nicely, are enraged by Facebook's silencing techniques you would be wrong!

Lo and behold, some from Europe's *anything goes* media had this to say:

Billionaire, alleged tax-dodger, CEO and all-round PC dullard Mark Zuckerberg has said Facebook is not doing enough to combat hate speech.

At a recent townhall event in Berlin he pledged to work closer with the German authorities, and even offered to fund a section of the German police, in order to help Facebook expand its view of "protected groups" and restrict "hate speech against migrants".

Pardon my German, but what utter scheisse.

What Zuckerberg seems to be missing is that Facebook is supposed to be about enabling the free interaction of people – all this talk of 'protected groups' and 'hate speech' should be anathema to him. But Zuckerberg subscribes to the typical metropolitan, Silicon-Valley-via-Ivy-League brand of faux-liberalism, which actually has a lot in common with the fascism he claims to despise.

"Hate speech has no place on Facebook or in our community", he said. "Until recently in Germany I don't think we were doing a good enough job, and I think we will continue needing to do a better and better job."

But how exactly is Zuckerberg, or anyone else, going to decide what hate speech is? It's just as subjective as, say, people's favourite songs. Just as one person's "Stairway to Heaven" might be another's "Birdie Song", so one person's call for controlled migration is another's idea of a Nuremberg speech.

Maybe you think we should open the borders, or maybe you think we should turn the boats back. The point is, both opinions (and all in between) have exactly the same right to be aired on the streets, on campuses and, yes, even on Facebook.

Believing in free speech means that everyone, whether they are a member of PEGIDA or Unite Against Fascism, should be entitled to express their view. They should also be prepared to be heavily criticized for their opinions. But they should not be silenced because a government, or a tech billionaire, disagrees with them.

In a truly free society there would be no "protected groups" and there would be no bans on "hate speech". Just because you approve of who the iron fist is punching today does not mean you are protected from receiving a ferrous uppercut tomorrow. [12]

In a word: wow!

Consequently, Facebook's machinations, in collaboration with the pro-Islamist and Marxist leadership of President Obama and various anti-freedom leaders, as they align with others within their own echo chamber - in one way or another, will eventually be revealed as a contributory factor to the bloodiest war imaginable.

For when the main mission (and the reasons are manifold) of the aforementioned is one and the same, to shield those whose anti-western actions are in plain view, how much distance can they place between themselves and nihilistic believers who are seeking to arm themselves with WMD's, the most lethal weapons known to man? Besides, what other outcome should they expect? As is said, the stage has been set.

PART TWO — THE EVIDENCE AGAINST FACEBOOK

HOW FACEBOOK DEALS WITH PAGES AND GROUPS OPPOSED TO MILITANT JIHAD VERSUS HOW IT DEALS WITH PAGES AND GROUPS SUPPORTING IT

N o discussion of Facebook and militant jihad would be complete without a thorough examination of the methods used by Facebook to enable those who long for a global Islamic caliphate while at the same time restricting and silencing those who oppose it.

Over the last several years, the social media giant has employed a number of tactics to silence dissent. The primary tactic, of course, remains what Internet users have long referred to as the *ban hammer*. Step out of line, say one wrong thing, and the hapless user is relegated to the blackest darkness of Internet "hell" where there is weeping, wailing and gnashing of teeth. We'll take a look at some examples of how Facebook enables jihad by telling the stories of pages, groups and users who have endured Facebook's wrath.

UNCLE SAM'S MISGUIDED CHILDREN

In July 2013, a very popular pro-veteran page named Uncle Sam's Misguided Children was mysteriously unpublished by Facebook. At the time, the page boasted over 600,000 supporters with readers worldwide. The page was well known for its hard-edged commentary and politically incorrect memes, many of which were aimed straight at militant Islam. Keep in mind the intended audience were veterans and those who support them. Facebook decided to unpublish the page, telling owner Rick Ferran it contained hate speech and nudity.[1] After personally reviewing the content, which was still available to administrators, of which I, Joe Newby, was made one for the purposes of my reporting, I was able to determine that Facebook's moderators either needed a refresher course in English or were playing fast and loose with the facts.

There was no nudity, although the page had pictures of attractive women in bikinis. The page was brought back up for a short time but was unpublished within hours. Ferran, a veteran of the United States Marine Corps who escaped Castro's Cuba, wasn't fazed, and proceeded to create another page. That too was torn down. This pattern has continued for the last two and a half years.

Ferran is now on the fourth version of the page, and has also had two very large groups closed down. Additionally, he has been personally slapped by Facebook with multiple bans and punishments. One of the most recent was a ban for being "insensitive."[2]

ISLAM EXPOSED (THE TRUTH ABOUT MILITANT ISLAM)

In June 2014, another page, Islam Exposed (The Truth about Militant Islam), was unpublished after Facebook claimed the page included pornographic content. Again, this author was given administrative rights to see the page and verify that it contained no such content.

Page administrators sent a letter to Facebook that contained screen shots of the page to prove that no such content existed. Page owners went on to say that "there is not one post that even closely resembles pornography to support the serious yet bogus, defamatory, and libelous charge made about it in the report, which resulted in Facebook's inexplicable decision to revoke our page."

Page owners, the letter added, even paid for advertising with the goal of increasing the page's reach. Instead of increasing viewers, they said, the page actually lost supporters. "The fact that our numbers have continued to drop rather than rise, despite our recently placed ad, suggests internal issues that, at the very least, surmount to misrepresentation and false advertising of services on the part of Facebook," the letter said.

Just prior to this, Facebook yanked the page but restored it, claiming that it was the result of a *mistake*. At that time, page administrators received death threats from critics but those threats were dismissed by Facebook. Instead of dealing with the threats leveled at administrators, Facebook chose to tear the page down, citing "harassment." In short, Facebook punished the victims for being threatened.

"A single bullet will strike ur (sic) head one day [admin] from a jihadist. Insha-Allah," one threat read. Another user with a Muslim-sounding name threatened to cut off administrators' heads if they continued to post articles in a rant too profane to quote here. Yet another person threatened to blackmail one of the administrators.

One administrator even received threatening phone calls. Those calls, he said, were reported to police, but nothing was done. Some of the threats were serious enough to report to authorities in the United States and Israel.

Facebook, however, continued to ignore the threats, page owners said. Worse yet, the site began targeting the page with what administrators called "harassment and censorship."

One post banned by Facebook asked users to refrain from posting anti-Muslim or hateful comments. This, Facebook decided, violated their murky community standards.

"This is not a Muslim hate page, as stated in our mission here. We hate the ideology of Islam and the brutality it perpetrates and condones," the post said. Visitors were also told to not use derogatory or threatening language. Page owners made it clear that such language does not help their mission to educate visitors.

Nevertheless, Facebook said the post violated their standards and the administrator who posted it received a thirty-day ban.

The page still exists, but now sits in a form of Facebook "purgatory," accessible only to administrators and another has been created to take its place. [3]

BRITAIN FIRST

Pushing the envelope of censorship even further, Facebook went after a page belonging to Britain First, a right-of-center British political party that is unapologetically patriotic and highly critical of what many now call an *invasion* of migrants from Middle-Eastern countries.

In December 2015, Facebook yanked the page with no explanation, prompting the party to label Facebook "fascist" and threaten lawsuits. At the time, the UK Independent quoted page owners who said that pulling the page "means that our 1.1 million supporters have been denied freedom of speech and expression." Moreover, the Party said it would establish "an immediate legal fund to drag Facebook into court."

Facebook backed down after the uproar and restored the page. According to reports, the political party was in talks with Facebook to determine why the page was pulled in the first place and Facebook claimed it was investigating the action. [4]

WE DO NOT WANT ISLAM IN THE CZECH REPUBLIC

In early January, the *Prague Monitor* reported that Facebook pulled the page for what some say is the Czech Republic's most-supported non-governmental group, or NGO. According to the report, the group had been accused of *extremism* and *xenophobia*, the Orwellian accusations often hurled at those who oppose militant Islamic jihad. Page owners rejected the accusations, and said they reject Islam and support free speech, the report said. [5] The page was blocked by Facebook last June, but owners said they were able to convince the social media company that opposition to Islamic ideology is not the same as fomenting hatred for individual Muslims.

The latest ban, however, may be more serious, said administrator and group chairman Dr. Martin Konvicka, a South Bohemian entomologist. "All of us know about the calls by many European politicians, including German Chancellor (Angela) Merkel and Czech Interior Minister (Milan) Chovanec (Social Democrats, CSSD), for censorship of social networks," he said.

Others also say the page was pulled as the result of false reports made by critics. A new page has been set up to replace the old one, but if the experience of others has indicated, it's only a matter of time before that one is also yanked.

ISRAEL'S INTELLECTUAL WARRIORS

Israel's Intellectual Warriors was a group started by Dr. Martin Sherman, a highly respected columnist with the Jerusalem Post whose work is widely regarded by Israeli decision-makers, Israel-friendly foreign policy circles and the Israeli public.

He served for seven years in operational capacities in the Israeli Defense establishment and was a ministerial adviser in a previous Israeli administration. Additionally, he is the founder and executive director of the Israel Institute for Strategic Studies. His group quickly reached about 4,000 members and was growing rapidly when it came under attack. "Late one night," he said, "the group was subjected to a massive attack by Arab/Muslims forces who had infiltrated the group. They posted highly distasteful images of hardcore porn and appalling horror scenes of dismembered bodies."

Dr. Sherman said he immediately began removing the offensive material when he spotted it the next day, but was already too late. Facebook, he added, "perversely and irrationally, removed the group, thus punishing the victim and not the perpetrators!! Numerous and repeated appeals, both from myself and many outraged members, to reverse the scandalous and senseless decision received no response and were utterly ignored, disregarded." This, unfortunately, is an old story that has been repeated over and over again.

ARAB ATHEIST NETWORK, ET.AL

In February 2016, the Council of Ex-Muslims of Britain posted a petition in which it said that some nineteen separate Facebook groups and pages were either torn down or currently under attack in the same way that Dr. Sherman's group was.[6]

The group said in its petition that it consists of former Muslims and free-thinkers who left Islam after researching it further, but cannot publicize their decision as they still live in the Middle East and would be subjected to beheading by religious extremists or harsh treatment under religious laws in their home country. The only outlet they have for interaction is social media sites like Facebook.

But, they added, Muslim fundamentalists and extremists didn't leave them alone, and created groups with thousands of followers who regularly reported their accounts and groups in an effort to close them. Facebook, they said, believed the false reports and closed down a number of the pages without any warning. Ten of their largest groups were shut down, they said in an appeal to Westerners who still value freedom of expression. The group even went so far as to suggest that Facebook may be in violation of international law, specifically, the International Covenant on Civil Rights and Political Rights, the Preamble of which says that, "the ideal of free human beings enjoying civil and political freedom and freedom from fear and want can only be achieved if conditions are created whereby everyone may enjoy his civil and political rights, as well as his economic, social and cultural rights . . . "

Article one of that document states: "All peoples have the right of self-determination. By virtue of that right they freely determine their political status and freely pursue their economic, social and cultural development." Article eighteen further says that, "Everyone shall have the right to freedom of thought, conscience and religion. This right shall include freedom to have or to adopt a religion or belief of his choice, and freedom, either individually or in community with others and in public or private, to manifest his religion or belief in worship, observance, practice and teaching."

Nowhere does the document say that those rights are subject to enforcement under Facebook's community standards.

The very next article adds: "Everyone shall have the right to hold opinions without interference." "Everyone shall have the right to freedom of expression; this right shall include freedom to seek, receive and impart information and ideas of all kinds, regardless of frontiers, either orally, in writing or in print, in the form of art, or through any other media of his choice," which obviously would include the Internet and sites like Facebook.

That document was first adopted by the General Assembly in 1966, and went into force in 1976, many years before Facebook was created.[7] Apparently, Mark Zuckerberg didn't get the memo.

In 2013, the website American Thinker reported that Facebook cracked down on no less than forty counter-jihad and patriot pages over a two-week period of time. The primary reason for the actions, Paul Murphy said at the time, was false claims of sexual content – a very common accusation leveled at conservative critics of jihad. "And because Facebook is free it simply won't have the manpower to check all reports. Thus it will ban indiscriminately -- on reports alone. Either that, or the Muslims and Leftists who work for Facebook are taking matters into their own hands by imposing Sharia Blasphemy Law on Facebook without its owners, or those at the top level, knowing this," Murphy wrote. [8]

Compare that to the treatment meted out to pages supportive of militant jihad.

We already discussed the experiment conducted by Shurat HaDin that documented Facebook's bias on video. Facebook ultimately pulled the anti-Israel page, but only after the video was seen by over a million users. This is an old story.

At about the same time as Murphy's report, a Facebook page promoting the beheading of *infidels* was flourishing. Worse yet, despite its blatantly violent content, Facebook refused to pull the page, telling those who filed reports that it did not violate their community standards. [9]

"When we Muslims take over America, you infidels will show respect or die," one person wrote on the page. At the time, then-Facebook spokesman Fred Wolens said in an email that there are different standards around images versus text. Oddly enough, that standard doesn't seem to apply to pages or individuals critical of Islam.

"Under our terms, this Page does not credibly threaten a specific person or target a protected category," he added, which might make one wonder whether or not average users who oppose militant jihad are considered deserving of protection. Robert Spencer disagreed with Facebook's assessment, calling it a page that promotes "real hatred and incitement to violence."

"It is not 'hate' when it's a Facebook page. It only becomes 'hate' when I report about it," he wrote at the time. [10]

Facebook ultimately pulled the page, but not before the chilling double standard was revealed. [11]

OTHER INSTANCES

This is hardly an isolated incident, as Walid Shoebat, Spencer and others have reported.

In December 2015, The Middle East Media Research Institute (MEMRI) reported that an Iranian Facebook account openly recruited Muslim youths in South Asia for jihad in Syria. [12]

In 2013, Shoebat reported on the case of Chiheb Esseghaier, the man charged with conspiring to derail a VIA passenger train in Canada.

According to Shoebat, Esseghaier's Facebook page displayed a "detailed flowchart on Al-Qaeda's plans, command and control, and methodology – from leadership to cell creation."

The page was deleted minutes later, he added, but not before it was captured for posterity. Facebook, it seems, got it right that time.[13]

Unfortunately, that's not always the case.

In 2014, World Net Daily (WND) reported that attorney Larry Klayman asked the Supreme Court to review a case that accused Facebook of allowing the posting of death threats against Jews. According to the report, Klayman said Facebook and CEO Mark Zuckerberg "failed to prevent what he found to be objectionable statements, including 'death threats against all Jews,' on the Third Intifada Page, which has more than 300,000 followers."

Facebook, he told WND, was asked to take the page down, but the company refused. "Only in the last few days did they do so, after increased pressure was exerted by the Israeli government. However, the damage had already been done and it is believed that this and other pages will soon reappear on Facebook," he added.

Indeed, as the lawsuit by Shurat HaDin indicates, those pages have returned and as usual, they get very little notice from Facebook until public pressure is applied.[14] Individual users, as we will demonstrate next, can also find themselves on the wrong end of what can only be called Facebook's double standard.

CHAPTER FIVE

HOW FACEBOOK TREATS USERS OPPOSED TO MILITANT JIHAD VERSUS THOSE WHO SUPPORT IT

In 2012, a Facebook user who wished to be identified only as *Marie*, logged into Facebook and was presented with a number of graphic death threats and threats of rape from individuals with Middle Eastern-sounding names. "We will kill you," one message read. Marie, naturally, was more than just a little concerned.

Being a responsible Facebook user, she reported the threats to Facebook. The response she got was jaw-dropping, to say the least. The social media giant sent her a private email saying the company could not confirm the threats violated their community standards.[1]

"We want people to feel safe when using Facebook," the company says on its Community Standards page. The site also states that "something that may be disagreeable or disturbing to you may not violate our Community Standards." Does that extend to threats of death and rape?

Regarding threats of violence, the site adds:

"We carefully review reports of threatening language to identify serious threats of harm to public and personal safety. We remove credible threats of physical harm to individuals. We also remove specific threats of theft, vandalism, or other financial harm."

Marie would tend to disagree. Making matters worse, she said the posts remained live for months afterward.

Make no mistake; Marie is not alone.

One co-author of this book experienced something quite similar, starting in mid-2014 and continuing well into 2015. A slew of private messages entered her Facebook inbox during that time, causing her a great deal of concern. One after another, the threats poured in and centered around one central theme: Stop all writings and interviews about Islam! If not, we will deal with you. We are coming after you! Israel and America will be destroyed!

At the same time, those posting the threats upped the ante and circulated her profile picture on Facebook. It made the rounds elsewhere, but it has yet to be definitively determined just how far and wide it was circulated. Worse yet, they cropped a crosshair (See Appendix A, Exhibit 11) into it, in an effort to punctuate their menacing intent. At the same time, they used this defaced photo as a *calling card* of sorts, and created a short video clip with an attached virus. Not only that, they sent it to countless pro-American and pro-Israel aligned contacts found on her Facebook page.

Not satisfied with their campaign of harassment and threats, one *friend* request after another kept popping up. There were so many requests that it was impossible to keep count. A decision was made to analyze the first dozen or so pages. Each one was part of the same Iranian *government* assemblage, so much so that they listed the Revolutionary Guards as their *work* place. As expected, their writings were (mostly) in Persian, therefore, Google translate had to suffice.

Three top-notch counterterrorism specialists independently analyzed samples of the threats and agreed they were real and not the work of *pranksters*. Working independently of each other, all three traced and verified the offending accounts. A few of the accounts, they found, were based in Saudi Arabia. The threats stopped once contact was made with enough of these militant jihadists, but the *friend* requests kept coming! Alas, one may rightfully inquire: Why not just turn off all requests from certain regions? The flipside became: How can we track this one and that one, and know with whom we are dealing, if those individuals are blocked? Basically, Sun Tzu's, "keep your friends close, and your enemies closer" was chosen as the wisest course of action. As is so often the case, Facebook took no action and did not even bother responding even after she filled out all the required forms. Sadly, this is a story that has been repeated over and over again.

Consider Pamela Geller, president of the American Freedom Defense Initiative (AFDI) and Stop Islamization of America (SIOA). Geller said she has been threatened so many times by Islamists on Facebook that she no longer bothers reporting the incidents. The reason for that is simple: Facebook, despite its high-minded community standards, does absolutely nothing.

In one recent incident, a Muslim detractor posted what can only be seen as a threat on her Facebook page. According to this individual, there is no freedom to "insult" Islam, nor is there any right to draw Muhammad.[2] But, he added, if there is a freedom to insult Islam, then there is freedom to kill those who do. The individual continued, warning Geller and others that everyone essentially must think as he does or be murdered.

We checked out this individual's page and found he had no friends and had made no posts. The profile appears to have been one created for the sole purpose of issuing threats on Geller's page. That is hardly the only threat Geller has received. According to an article she published on Breitbart.com, calls to "rape and dice" her regularly appear on Facebook.[3]

"I am sick and tired of the suppression of our speech," she wrote. "We are unable to engage in the public square. And yes, Facebook is the public square; it's where we connect. We have to fight for it. Shouting into the wilderness is not freedom of speech." Geller says that like so many others, she is repeatedly threatened, warned and punished for reporting about radical Islam, Sharia oppression and violent jihad.

Meanwhile, CEO Mark Zuckerberg recently assured Muslims that Facebook would be a safe and welcoming place for them. That is all well and good, but what about everyone else?[4]

Facebook's Orwellian treatment of counter-jihad supporters goes even further. One co-author of this book has written a number of articles regarding Facebook's actions as well as stories covering terrorism and the actions of those who support Sharia law and militant jihad.

Starting in May 2015, the site began to punish him by attributing comments and links he never posted. From May to December 2015, he was slapped with no less than six separate bans, all over posts he never made. Worse yet, the posts were formatted in such a way as to appear that he made them when he didn't. Adding insult to injury, the bans were perfectly timed to coincide within days, or even hours, of the previous ban.

Several others said they were banned for the exact same posts – each one also made to appear as though they posted them. After blogger Faye Higbee wrote about the phenomenon, even more came forward to say they, too, had been similarly banned.[5] One counter-jihadist called the incident *Forgegate* and said he had been banned for the exact same post Facebook used against the co-author.

In 2013, Examiner.com's Christopher Collins, citing various reports from multiple sites, said an Islamic group posted a $500,000 bounty against an administrator of a counter-jihad Facebook page. The page, "Ban Islam," had been removed by Facebook thanks in part to a deluge of complaints from a group known as Islamic Socialist Network, he reported.[6] "It appears that the Islamic Socialist Network has created a 'Hit List' of Counter jihad web pages to attack," said Schuyler Montague. "And, if this wasn't bad enough, we discovered this hit list also extends to the administrators of these web pages, as well."

Thanks to the hard work of Montague and others, many of the pages involved were finally removed, but one has to ask: How many more like it are out there? And how many other counter-jihadists have suffered Facebook's Orwellian actions and simply suffered in silence?

Shortly after that article was published, Collins said Facebook slapped him with a ban.

A series of posts dating back to 2014 and later made public by the *Bare Naked Islam* blog gives the reader a sense of the type of thing Facebook is willing to tolerate from militant Islamists.[7] "[D]ie u kuffar bastard (sic)," one Facebook message read. The user threatened an owner of "Our Eye on Islam" with rape and death if the page continued displaying anti-jihad posts. Ironically, the user said Islam means "peace and tolerance among other people."

"Is it so hard to say Islam means peace," the offended Muslim asked. When presented with the hypocrisy of his own words, he let the cat out of the bag by telling the administrator, "you won't be raped or killed" as long as "you don't insult Islam."

But the poster was far from being finished. He went on to say that Islam "wouldn't exist today" without murder and rape. Sometimes, he wrote, "it's necessary to kill the kuffar and rape their women," which he said is the only way to please Allah. Imagine, just for a moment, the outrage that would ensue if those words were written by anyone else. The man later whined when others began circulating his offensive screeds and demanded they be deleted.

In December 2015, a manager for the popular "Restless Patriots" Facebook page said she was given a thirty-day ban after posting a picture of San Bernardino shooter Tashfeen Malik. The picture also presented a simple question: "Presidential candidate Donald Trump is calling for 'a total and complete shutdown of Muslims entering the United States until our country's representatives can figure out what is going on. Do you agree?'"[8]

Facebook's moderators took offense and tore the picture down while banning the page owner. Ironically, Malik pledged allegiance to ISIS on Facebook shortly before being killed in the terrorist attack. Facebook, it seems, had no problem with that.

Another Examiner.com contributor, Renee Nal, noted:

In a recent interview with Sean Hannity, Jennifer Thalasinos, the widow of a victim of last week's terror attack in San Bernardino Nicholas Thalasinos, commented that her husband - a conservative that she believes was targeted for his views by the Muslim shooters - was previously targeted on Facebook, resulting in him being blocked for extended periods of time . . .James Neighbors, the founder of the popular "Overpasses for America" Facebook page told the Examiner that he has been placed in the "Facebook Gulag" "4 or 5 times in 2015 alone . . ." Neighbors said that he "spent essentially 4 of the last 6 months locked down for the most frivolous of offenses." [9]

The same month, gun rights activist and writer Jan Morgan was slapped with a thirty-day ban after writing a post Fox Business said was critical of letting *Sharia-compliant Muslims* into the United States. According to Facebook, Morgan was guilty of repeatedly posting things that violate their community standards.

Morgan then used her husband's account to let fans know what happened and to inform them she would be discussing the issue on Fox Business. That post was also removed by Facebook. Facebook relented, saying it was all a mistake, but the ban was not lifted until the company was told of her network appearance. Morgan responded, telling Facebook she hears of this kind of treatment from conservatives across the country.[10]

In January 2016, another female Facebook user was the target of extremely graphic and profane threats from an individual with a Middle Eastern-sounding name. "I will feast on the blood of your family," the individual said in one of the very few statements fit to print. The perpetrator also posted threats to kill and behead members of the woman's family.

The woman filed a complaint with Facebook and was promptly told the violent threats did not violate their community standards.

"Please let us know if you see anything else that concerns you," Facebook said. "We want to keep Facebook safe and welcoming for everyone."[11]

Everyone, apparently, except those who oppose violent Islamic jihad. One would think the FBI might be interested in looking into these threats, but it seems they're far too busy these days investigating bacon on the door handles of mosques.[12]

Later that same month, Facebook banned blogger and activist Christopher Cantwell for a post supporting victims of migrant rape.[13] According to Cantwell, the post decried the victims of a New Year's Eve *rapefest* in Germany. Cantwell observed that he had never made the post, yet it was formatted to appear as though he had.

"I am not sure why Facebook opted to show it to me in this context," he wrote. "All admins of the [We Like Gun Rights] page received the same notice, but with their own name and profile picture being shown as the poster." The page was also unpublished for a time, he added, but was later restored. Cantwell issued a dire warning. "This is a troubling trend that seems to get worse by the day. The Internet had once provided us with a means of breaking from mainstream media narratives and giving each individual a voice," he said. "But, as political correctness and government (policies) bring pressure to bear on popular online gathering places, that is ceasing to be the case. Expressing political opinions that run contrary to PC narratives or government policy will now get you silence on the most popular platforms and as internet regulations steadily increase we can expect this to also come at the ISP level."

Adding to the list of the *banned and damned* is Michael Savage. In late 2015, WND reported that talk-radio host Michael Savage was banned after he dared to post photographs of the February 3, 2006, demonstration held outside the Embassy of Denmark in London.

According to the report, the focus of protest was the publication of cartoons depicting Muhammad in the Danish newspaper *Jyllands-Posten*. Snopes.com verified the photographs were taken at the

London demonstration, with one exception which was taken at a protest in the English city of Luton. Shortly afterward, Facebook removed his post, claiming the social media site "determined that it violated Facebook community standards."[14]

Is there a double standard? Facebook executives and spokespeople repeatedly and routinely say they support freedom of expression and give each reported case equal treatment. But as the old saw goes, actions speak louder than words.

CHAPTER SIX

HOW FACEBOOK HAS DEALT WITH ARTICLES AND LINKS CRITICAL OF MILITANT JIHAD

Facebook has a literal arsenal of online weapons it can use to stifle news and information it deems to be offensive. We've discussed the use of some of those tools in previous chapters, but Facebook has also found creative ways to squash articles that deal with topics like militant jihad.

In May 2014, Dave Gaubatz, a highly respected counterterrorism specialist who co-authored *Muslim Mafia*, said he infiltrated a Muslim conference held in Detroit earlier in the month.[1]

"I was recently at an ISNA Conference. The executive leaders essentially said they have Facebook leaders in their 'pockets'," he said, referring to the Islamic Society of North America, an organization that is a top Muslim Brotherhood front group within North America.

According to Gaubatz, an individual who identified himself as a representative of Muslim Advocates reportedly told him the group is "working closely" with social media sites like Facebook and Twitter to close down accounts of users critical of Islam.

"This is considered serious hate speech and should not be allowed on the Internet," Gaubatz explained. The representative also reportedly said that "anyone critical of Islam and sharia law are haters." The same description applied to those who oppose the construction or expansion of mosques in the United States, he added.

Given the seriousness of the charge, the author reached out to both Facebook and the Muslim Advocates seeking comment. Facebook, and this happens more often than not, did not respond to the author's request.

Fatima Khan, executive director of the organization, responded with a friendly, albeit useless message containing standard public relations boilerplate. Unfortunately, Khan's message came too late as the article had already been published.

About two hours later, Khan responded. Her tone after reading the article had changed somewhat as she apparently thought she could intimidate the author into pulling the article by using the standard, "Who is your editor?" tactic. After being informed that the article did not attribute anything to her representative directly, and presented with a second opportunity to directly respond to the writer's questions, she cut off contact. It is interesting to note, however, that she neither confirmed nor denied Gaubatz's allegations.

Shortly after that exchange the article was flagged by Facebook as *unsafe*. Facebook did not explain what, exactly made the article unsafe, and the timing, coming as it did so soon after the exchange with Khan, was highly suspect. Did Khan have a direct connection to someone at Facebook's enforcement arm? The evidence, although circumstantial, would suggest to a reasonable and logical person that may be the case.

This was not an isolated incident, however. Another article written shortly after that got the same treatment and an article published in 2015 was similarly flagged within twenty minutes of being posted to Facebook. The only thing these articles had in common was the topic: Islam.[2]

Gadi Adelman, a counterterrorism expert who contributes to the Jerusalem Post, said Facebook has done the same thing with links to his articles. The problem, he explained, began in January 2014 and had been ongoing as of June of that same year.[3]

Dr. Martin Sherman, the highly acclaimed *Jerusalem Post* columnist we introduced in a previous chapter, produces a weekly article under his column, and told us he is repeatedly banned from posting or joining in groups, despite the fact that his material is *generally welcome* in the groups where he posts. As usual, the bans often come without warning or explanation.

In February 2014, Eliot Higgins, a visiting research associate at King's College London, said he was looking into a sarin gas attack that took place the previous year, but was unable to find any information. Thanks to the social media site's censorship, he tweeted, ". . .nearly every Facebook page reporting on the attack is gone . . ." Because Facebook deleted nearly all of the pages by Syrian opposition groups, vital information about the conflict in the region has been lost.[4]

Speaking to *The Atlantic*, Richard Allan, Facebook's director of public policy for Europe, the Middle East, and Africa, admitted the company's reporting system isn't perfect and acknowledged that human error does cause pages and posts to be deleted when they shouldn't be. What locals regard as news stories, he explained, the company could see as offensive.

Dlshad Othman, a Syrian digital-security expert and cyberactivist, told *The Atlantic* that Facebook, oddly enough, "used to be proud that it was part of the Arab Spring."[5]

Facebook's actions, allegedly part of an effort to combat *hate*, not only undermine the basic concept of a free and open press, they are having real consequences for those seeking to bring justice for victims of war crimes in the Middle East.

Facebook said that pages or stories are not taken down until they have been reviewed by an actual human being. This means that all of the incidents we have reported were apparently taken after someone had physically looked at the article. As Felim McMahon posted in 2014, these deletions are having a major impact on reporting from the area, as well as efforts to document alleged criminal behavior on the part of the Syrian government.

"From a journalistic point of view, Facebook pages that helped Storyful corroborate some of the most important content from Syria have been removed from the public domain," he said. "Most alarming of all is the suggestion here that there is little scrutiny of complaints that lead to the closures, and little recourse for those who find themselves censored."[6]

Now the company has embarked on a crusade to eliminate what it views as *hate* from the entire European continent.[7] The move was announced by Chief Operations Officer Sheryl Sandberg, one of those responsible for the failed effort to ban "bossy" from the English language.[8]

The effort, titled the "Online Civil Courage Initiative," is allegedly about "combating extremism and hate speech on the Internet." "This is necessary because right-wing extremism, racism and anti-semitism are present in all walks of life in Germany," one spokesman said. But it wasn't *white pride skinheads* or neo-Nazis who engaged in a mass sexual assault spree in Germany on New Year's Eve. Nevertheless, the initiative purports to eventually purge Europe of all xenophobic rhetoric. The problem, however, is that Facebook didn't exactly define what constitutes *xenophobic rhetoric*. The initiative, *Reuters* reported in early 2016, appears to be in response to an investigation by German authorities who claimed Facebook wasn't doing enough to combat "hate speech" on its platform.

As a result, Breitbart.com called Facebook "the world's most dangerous censor," comparing it to the East German Stasi and Hitler's Gestapo.[9] "The future is here: not the one envisaged by Gene Roddenberry, but by George Orwell," wrote Allum Bokhari. "We all saw this coming," he added.

Indeed, those of us who have spent years documenting Facebook's actions have seen this level of censorship coming, but were dismissed as kooks and told to leave Facebook if we didn't approve of its actions. Many of those same critics aren't laughing now, as Facebook's actions are having a direct impact on a free press, one of the major underpinnings of a free society. These actions also enable militant Islamic jihadists who could be excused for thinking that media reports of their activity would be censored by the social media giant.

CHAPTER SEVEN

FACEBOOK'S COUNTERTERROR EFFORTS: CLOSING THE BARN DOOR AFTER THE HORSES HAVE ESCAPED

Non-tainted investigative journalists have hardly been impressed by Facebook's implementation of a so-called "counterterrorism squad." In a word: hogwash. This co-author's counterterror and counter intelligence sources are equally unfazed. One such PR report, titled, "Facebook vs ISIS: Inside The Tech Giant's Antiterror Strategy," is excerpted as follows:

> *In a rare interview with Yahoo News, Monica Bickert, a former federal prosecutor who serves as Facebook's top content cop, provided the company's most detailed accounting yet of its efforts to identify and remove terrorist material from its site. As described by Bickert, Facebook has set up what amounts to its own counterterrorism squad, with at least five offices around the world and scores of specialists fluent in several dozen languages.*

> *The group, part of Facebook's Community Operations team, responds around the clock to reports by Facebook users and others of terrorists using the social media network, taking terror-related material down — and then looking for related accounts that the same actors might be using. "If we become aware of an account that is supporting terrorism, we'll remove that account," said*

Bickert, chief of global policy management, in an interview at Facebook's sprawling campus in Menlo Park, Calif. "But we want to make sure that we get it all. So we will look at associated accounts — pages this person liked or groups that he may have belonged to — and make sure that we are moving all associated violating content." Facebook — which now has 1.5 billion users, 70 percent of them outside the United States and Canada — is not only looking for messages or posts from avowed members of the Islamic State or other terror groups, Bickert says. It has instituted community standards policies — controversial in some circles — that go beyond those of other social media firms, banning expressions of "support" for terrorist groups and expressions "praising" their leaders or "condoning" violent terrorist acts. "If there is a terror attack that happens in the world, and somebody shares even a news report of that and says, 'I think this is wonderful,' or they're mocking the victims or celebrating what has happened, that violates our policies and we'll remove it," said Bickert.[1]

Realistically speaking, Bickert's *rare interview* (along with the rest of Facebook's heavy-hitters) should be deemed little more than a stepped-up rendering of a fable and fairytale, spun from a highly compensated hired gun. It is that transparent.

For all practical purposes, if any of Facebook's associated spin is even remotely truthful and believable, how could it be that a logic-based, rational, and competent "Community Operations" department - overseen by a newly appointed "Counterterror Squad", no less - mistook the following page (cited below) for the real (ISIS) thing? After all, a crucial part of due diligence mandates an across the board application of critical analysis, some of which involves monitoring, engaging, testing, digging beneath the surface, screening, sampling, and then eliminating. Stipulated, some situations are patently obvious, like those containing jihadi paraphernalia, videos, and written content. On the other side of the spectrum, the remainder requires various methods of testing to ensure that a correct analysis and outcome prevails. By the way, this is Counterterrorism 101.

According to a report titled, "Facebook Is Joining the Fight Against Terrorism – One Woman Named Isis At A Time":

Isis Anchalee, an engineer based in San Francisco, complained on Twitter on Tuesday afternoon that her Facebook account had been disabled, and suggested it was because of her name.

"Why would you disable my personal account? MY REAL NAME IS ISIS ANCHALEE /facepalm," she tweeted at Facebook.

— Isis Anchalee (@isisAnchalee)

November 16, 2015

@facebook .... why? pic.twitter.com/F6BPvdRnep

One of her Facebook friends noted that their message thread had been marked as spam. "Facebook thinks I'm a terrorist and froze my account," she replied.

She said she sent Facebook a screenshot of her passport, proving that her birth name was Isis.

She said the third effort she made to verify her identity proved successful.

A Facebook researcher, Omid Farivar, tweeted at Anchalee publicly to apologise eight hours after her initial complaint on Tuesday. "Isis, sorry about this. I don't know what happened. I've reported it to the right people and we're working on fixing it."

Earlier this year Facebook cemented a policy requiring people to use their real names. Users are asked to refrain from adding symbols, punctuation, unusual characters, professional or religious titles, or "offensive or suggestive words of any kind" to their names to "keep our community safe."

But execution of that policy has been uneven, as Nadia Drake wrote in Wired in June.

Facebook's Safety Check Leads Technology's Support of Paris

'Part of the motivation is stopping the proliferation of celebrity imposter accounts and profiles made for pets. But it's also allowed Facebook to shutter the accounts of real people, based on 'authenticity'. What does 'authentic' mean, though? It's both confusing and contextual, because identity itself is confusing and contextual,' she wrote.

'Despite those complexities, Facebook believes it can determine authenticity for you.'

A Facebook spokesman told the Guardian the error was made as part of 'a fake account reporting process', and apologised for the trouble it caused. 'It was not connected to the individual's name and her account has already been restored.'

Anchalee did not respond to requests for comment. Anchalee told a reporter from Tech Insider that she wanted to avoid a 'media storm' over the issue: 'I just wanted my account back. [2]

Readers, you can't make this stuff up. But we are not done yet.

Then there's the alleged gold/money laundering case we discussed in Chapter Two. How could it be that under their embarrassingly heralded *Community Operations* department, paradoxically, overseen by a newly appointed *Counterterror Squad*, they missed what has been right under their *investigative* noses, hiding in plain sight?

Could it be that they are not as seriously interested in checking out *what's what* on their pages, by those who may, or may not, operate so-called legitimate businesses? After all, it is a *Counterterror Squad's* mandate to execute their due diligence and determine who's who.

Besides, how much heavy-lifting are these authors supposed to perform, being that we are not on Facebook's payroll! Alas, as we journey further down Facebook's rabbit hole, in an Alice in

Wonderland moment, another much touted program to counter online terrorist propaganda is heralded. Not so fast.

Called "Counter Speech," supposed free advertising is being offered to "those who use their Facebook platform to discredit extremist views, whether it's by use of text posts, images or video content. Those whose work is seen to dismantle propaganda will be rewarded with ad credits worth up to $1,000 (£691), helping them spread their reach even further."

More tellingly, "however, Counter Speech doesn't appear to be a program that users can apply to, but rather one where Facebook itself seeks out worthy candidates. One of the first recipients has been comedian Arbi el Ayachi, whose short videos counter Western stereotypes of Muslims and Islam.

The plan has been brewing in the background for a while. Monika Bickert, Facebook's head of global policy management, put the plan together in December 2015, reports The Wall Street Journal. Making anti-terrorism content more visible on Facebook has since become a concern at the company's highest levels, with CEO Sheryl Sandberg saying at Davos last month that a wave of positivity and goodwill could deter radicalization and terrorist recruitment online."[3]

In light of this fact, is it an exaggeration to assess that Facebook's *policing* strategy is more in league with Lewis Carroll's, *Through the Looking Glass*? When juxtaposed against real efforts conducted by counterterror and counterintelligence professionals who operate online to mitigate, frustrate, and interfere with the plots of Islamic terrorists, there is no comparison. As is known, you can't place lipstick on a pig and expect it not to look (and smell) like a pig.

But the situation is even worse than that. While Facebook was busy protecting the world from women named Isis, real terrorists were buying and selling military hardware on the social media site, despite Facebook's very clear prohibition against buying and selling guns!

In February 2016, the *Daily Mirror* reported that al Qaeda fighters were actually using the site to buy and sell "CIA weaponry."

One post showed an AGS-17 Soviet-Era grenade launcher available for a mere $3,800 while another post showed a TOW missile launcher the seller claimed came from the Pentagon.

TOW missiles, the *Daily Mirror* said, have been provided to Syrian rebel groups by the CIA for some time and it's believed one was used in an attack on an Egyptian Navy vessel in September 2015. MANPADs, missile systems capable of bringing down civilian and military aircraft, were also advertised for as much as sixty-seven thousand dollars.[4]

Facebook took down the page, but only after the *Mirror* inquired about it. It's not known if any of the information on the page was provided to defense analysts for further review.

As it turns out, guns aren't the only things terrorists buy and sell on Facebook. In late May, *The Washington Post* reported that ISIS extremists were also selling sex slaves on the social media giant for as much as eight thousand dollars.

"To all the bros thinking about buying a slave, this one is $8,000," said an ISIS fighter who calls himself Abu Assad Almani. The page was taken down by Facebook, but the incident reveals how much Islamic terrorists depend on social media.[5]

To reiterate, as this book has proven that instead of shutting down pages that incite and inspire others to commit jihad under the banner and sword of Allah, Facebook's denizens work assiduously toward silencing those whose sole aim is to expose said Islamic terror. Resultant, the looming question is: Why are Facebook's representatives bothering to create what amounts to a *dog and pony show* with the latest *Community Operations* team(s) assigned to block ISIS's efforts at the tech giant's platform?

Before we proceed, it is imperative to take note of the program's basis. Simply put, its main focus is on the Islamic State, as if ISIS is an anomaly which distorts the peaceful tenets of Islam. In other words, "ISIL" - as President Obama, his surrogates, and Islamists are wont to call it - is distinct verbiage that incontestably signals a wink and a nod to the overall Muslim ummah, in their aspiration to resurrect the seventh-century Mideast and global caliphate. Historically, ISIL encompasses the Islamic State in Iraq and the Levant. Resultant, it eliminates Israel, an "illegitimate" state in the eyes of the worldwide ummah and leftist enablers. Absolutely, lexicon matters. The point being, Facebook's counterterrorism hunters are tasked to dislodge and separate ISIS from Islam. Concomitantly, representatives, through their *rare* interviews, want to ensure that they drill this distinction without a difference into the public's consciousness. How's that working out?

Moreover, from a business perspective, their overall plan to anchor in place teams to monitor this and that makes perfect sense, in anticipation of shielding the company even further when class action lawsuits pick up steam. However, from a practical application standpoint, the program is useless and toothless. Take this professional assessment to the bank.

Not only that, as militant Islamic jihadists explode all over the west (recently engulfing Brussels, Paris, and Nice ultimately, setting their sights on nuclear power plants) and catapult at breakneck speed, Facebook (alongside other major platforms) will find itself in the crosshairs.

And speaking of the bloody carnage waged in Nice, France on July 14, 2016, an urgent question must be asked: where were Facebook's "counterterror squads" when Chokri C. in April 2016 sent the lead terrorist, Tunisian born Mohamed Lahouaiej Bouhlel, a Facebook message which read: "Load the truck with 2,000 tonnes of iron....release the brakes my friend and I will watch."

Pray tell, was this deemed unworthy of in-depth scrutiny and analysis by their much heralded and hard-charging "counterterror squads"? If so, why? More pointedly, why weren't Facebook's engineering wizards tasked - by the aforementioned forces - to plug in as many algorithms as necessary to capture said jihadi messaging? Along this same trajectory, one must rightfully inquire: isn't chasing after militant Islamic jihadists as intrinsic to Facebook's community standards as click-baits, you know, where algorithms are utilized to the umpteenth degree? Even more so, could it be that Muslim names are automatically relegated to a protective type of status, a policy of *hands-off* by the site's ever present *Ban and Boom* censorship monitors? Assuredly, victims (those who live to tell the tale) and their families will hold each and every enabling entity accountable for giving them *safe haven a la* the ubiquitous *sanctuary cities*, albeit online.

It gets worse. Knowing what you do about Facebook's *Counterterror Squad*, who wants to bet that ISIS's *classified ads* - found via the Deep Web - didn't make it onto Facebook's endless pages where militant Islamic jihadists comfortably congregate? Well, the advice within these pages is: it's a fool's wager! In March 2016, *Vocative* reported:

> *Wanted: Social media gurus to join an online outreach campaign that grows audiences and community participation. Must be into terrorism.*

> *ISIS forums posted several online vacancies in the past few days calling for strategists to join their online propaganda units that disseminate material to the terror group's supporters around the world. The forums were found by Vocativ's Deep Web analysts.*

> *Titled: "A call to Knights of Uploading," the job posts called for people who could multi-task, work under pressure, and have area expertise. "We want to bring back the division of labor and distribution of roles of the brothers and sisters," one post on ISIS' al-Minbar and Shumukh al-Islam forums read.*

> *"There many who have knowledge in this area, but get confused by multiple tasks and on what to work," the post said. "And even worse: they leave the work because of the pressure."*

> *The post lists seven possible positions and invite users to join "to support the Islamic State and provoke the enemies of Allah." The position includes working on YouTube, Twitter and Facebook accounts, "providing links to watch or download videos, publish*

on forums and social media networks," and link to news from ISIS' media arm, the Amaq news agency.

The post also includes technical instructions on how to upload videos to multiple cloud services at a time and provides a list of recommended sites supporters can use to upload videos. These are quick and don't require registration, the post notes.

ISIS has become increasingly savvy in its social media presence, using networks to disseminate its propaganda. Over the past few months, ISIS supporters have responded to efforts by Twitter to minimize its reach, instructing followers to move to other platforms such as the messaging app Telegram. Last month, Twitter said it suspended 125,000 accounts "for threatening or promoting terrorist acts, primarily related to ISIS." Facebook has said that it works to ensure that terrorists don't use the site, and that it removes content supporting terrorism.

A recent report by George Washington University's Program on Extremism said the amount of pro-ISIS content available on Twitter has been limited by account suspensions since last summer. Suspensions have also impacted the reach of specific ISIS-affiliated users who have been repeatedly targeted, the report said.[6]

We are not done yet. Alas, to possibly satisfy some *doubting Thomas'*, pay heed to the following (verifiable) claims and stats from ISIS, irrespective of Zuckerberg's gobbledygook. And more of the same applies to their hydra-related Muslim Brotherhood Mafia axis.

"Facebook's mission and what we really focus on giving everyone the power to share all of the things that they care about," Zuckerberg, the recipient of the first-ever Axel Springer Award for outstanding entrepreneur personality, told the media company's CEO, Mathias Döpfner, in an interview in Berlin on Thursday.

"What they're thinking about, what they're experiencing on a day-to-day basis, and the idea is that everyone has the power to share those things, then that makes the world more understanding, it helps people stay closer to the people who they love, all these good things that we value," gushed Zuckerberg.

That message seems to be taken to heart by Islamic State, despite efforts to exclude the group from Facebook's big happy family. A video posted earlier this week by the group's hacking unit "Sons Caliphate Army" said ISIS has more than 10,000 Facebook accounts, 150 Facebook groups and 5,000 Twitter accounts. "You are not in our league," the group said in a message addressed to Zuckerberg, Twitter CEO . . . Jack Dorsey and "their crusader government."

Another group of not-so-savory Facebook users is arms dealers. An investigation by IBTimes U.K. found that arms dealers across Egypt, Syria, Libya, Gaza and Iraq are using Facebook to sell weapons and missiles to pretty much anyone who wants to buy a weapon.

And it's not just the sale of tanks and terror. A Sunday People probe published last November found a 149% rise in serious crimes linked to social media, including murder, and blackmail, and pedophilia.

But an ever-cheerful Facebook went on a you-make-it-we-share-it binge earlier this month, marking its 12th birthday with #friendsay videos, personalized for every user. Imagine moments and pictures from the last year set to music that could be shared with one click."[7]

Even so, unlike Jews in Israel, few bear the brunt of the social media giant's enabling of militant Islamic jihadists, irrespective of Facebook representatives shrill claim: yes, their Counterterror Squads are in place!

More specifically, according to one security expert and former Knesset Member in Israel, Yoni Chetboun, such paradigms are indeed no longer relevant - and to defeat it, Israel's basic security doctrine must undergo a radical shift.

Yoni Chetboun, a one-time Jewish Home party MK and member of the Knesset Foreign Affairs and Defense Committee, has had a distinguished military career. He served for several years as a soldier, and then as an officer, in the IDF's elite Egoz counterterrorism unit, and took part in major operations in Judea, Samaria, Gaza and Lebanon. Chetboun was awarded the IDF Chief of Staff citation for his heroism during the Battle of Bint Jbeil during the 2006 Second Lebanon War.

After 10 years of active military service he left the army in 2008, but continued serving as an officer in the reserves - where he recently graduated as a Battalion Commander, receiving the senior rank of Lieutenant Colonel (sgan aluf) . . .

"There is no intelligence which can stop someone from picking up a knife from his kitchen and going out to kill a Jew after being incited on Facebook or hearing a sermon in his mosque on Friday," he added. In that sense "it is harder now than ever to take preventative action . . .[8]

And according to an analysis at the very highly reputable and on target Israeli intelligence agency, the Meir Amit Intelligence and Terrorism Information Center, "The social networks as a source of inspiration and imitation for terrorists: the case study of two Palestinian youths who carried out a stabbing attack in a supermarket in the commercial area of Sha'ar Benyamin", the following is more than germane. It is a bulls-eye.

1   *On February 18, 2016, Two Palestinian adolescents went to a supermarket in the Sha'ar Benyamin commercial area, north of Jerusalem, and stabbed two Israeli customers. An armed civilian shot them. One of the customers, a 21-year-old*

off-duty IDF soldier, was mortally wounded and later died. Another Israeli customer was critically wounded. The two youths were critically wounded and are in Israeli hospitals (one was mistakenly reported killed in the initial report).

2   *According to the initial investigation, the two walked around inside the supermarket for about 40 minutes before they carried out the attack. The Israeli customers were stabbed in two different sections of the store. A third Palestinian entered the store with the two terrorists and was held back by the security guard at the entrance. He was examined but no weapon was found in his possession.*

3   *The two terrorists who carried out the stabbing attack were Iham Sabah and Omar Samir Taha al-Rimawi, both14-years-old, from the village of Bituniya (west of Ramallah). The al-Rimawi family originally came from Bayt Rima (northeast of Ramallah). Iham Sabah was apparently religious and customarily went to the mosque to pray . . .*

4   *On February 21, 2016, Sultan Abu al-Einein, a member of Fatah's Central Committee, who is also Mahmoud Abbas' advisor for international organizations, posted a notice on his Facebook page glorifying and praising the action of the two terrorists. He wrote, "Iham [Sabah] and Omar [al-Rimawi], you are our leaders." He praised them saying, chronologically they were 14-years-old, but in reality each one was "tens of generations old." Within their chests, he said, "beat the hearts of [brave] men." Those hearts were angry because of the [spilled] blood of Ahmed Manasra (a13-year-old Palestinian who carried out a stabbing attack in the Pisgat Ze'ev neighborhood of Jerusalem) and Yasmin al-Zarou (al-Tamimi) (a14-year-old Palestinian girl from Hebron who carried out a stabbing attack at the Cave of the Patriarchs) . . .*

5   *It was not the first time during the current terrorist campaign that Sultan Abu al-Einein unequivocally expressed support for*

Palestinian terrorists carrying out attacks. For example, on October 4, 2015, on his Facebook page he praised Palestinians who carried out terrorist attacks, calling them "the candles that light the way to the altar of freedom." On November 5, 2015, he expressed support for the terrorist who carried out the vehicular attack in the Sheikh Jarrah neighborhood of Jerusalem (killing a Border Police officer and wounding 13 Israeli civilians and Border Policemen). In both instances, his Facebook postings received "likes" expressing encouragement and support for the shaheeds . . .

The Use of Facebook Pages by the Two Youths

6 *Both terrorists had Facebook pages. The Facebook page of Iham Sabah was created in April 2014 but was not particularly active. However, he did occasionally respond to messages posted by Omar al-Rimawi regarding a terrorist attack. The Facebook page of Omar al-Rimawi, which he created in 2012 when he was 11-years-old, was more active.[1] As of last year he posted notices supporting the shaheeds and expressing the desire to follow in their footsteps. Such posts became more frequent in September 2015, at about the time the current terrorist campaign began . . .*₉

Similarly, advance notice was given via Facebook (hours before another attack, among a continuous list in Israel), this time in January 2016.

The terrorist was revealed to be a PA police officer, who previously worked as the personal bodyguard of the attorney general of the PA in Ramallah, Samaria.

Hours before the attack, he wrote on Facebook: "good morning, I will become a shahid (martyr) and join Allah and his messenger Mohammed. This is a morning of victory!" The terrorist was shot dead in the attack.[10]

Most tellingly, how is it possible that an Israeli NGO is reduced to begging Facebook: Stop killing Jews!?

An Israeli NGO launched a crowdfunding initiative . . . on Sunday soliciting donations in order to subsidize billboards to be placed near the home of Facebook founder Mark Zuckerberg as a form of protest for indulging Palestinian incitement on the popular social media tool.

In a YouTube video, the Shurat Hadin – Israel Law Center criticized Zuckerberg for failing to crack down on Palestinian incitement while calling him to task for "supporting Muslims" in a previous post.

"When Palestinian terrorists called for the killing of Jews on Facebook, Facebook closed its eyes," the narrator of the video says as an image of Zuckerberg with his eyes shut is displayed.[11]

Mirroring many business behemoths whose views are seen from a hugely distorted multicultural lens, it is impossible for Facebook's top leadership to be anything other than "neutral". This is true even when it entails the bloody ravaging of soldiers for Allah, as they gallop across the globe. Realistically, how can they be expected to rein them in without the court of public opinion forcing them to? Most significantly, their collective view of militant Islamic jihadists can be summed up under the general worldview: They are *misunderstood* for being the "other", hence, deserving of the west's sympathy! It is insane, but no less true.

At its base, regardless of the name of the person repping for Facebook, any claim that the site is waging an all-out effort to stop ISIS or any other terror hydra from exploiting the platform is simply untrue. They should be given the same credence as if Facebook put forth the following press release: "We have concluded that the moon is made of green cheese, therefore, just trust that we conducted our proper due diligence by hiring the best experts that money can buy, and that is that." Afterwards, visualize, in your mind's eye, Hillary

Clinton's infamous statement, "What difference at this point does it make"[12] anyway? Precisely.

But if a comparative analysis is called for, the notion that Facebook, despite hiring professionals who are (more than likely) duly versed in employing the necessary tools of the trade, has suddenly woken up and is prepared to rein in terrorists who run rampant within the site, it is akin to closing the barn door after the horses have escaped. Ahhh, indeed, what difference does it make to hire this one and that one, after millions upon millions of militant Islamic jihadists have already escaped and plotted, even before their *counterterror teams* arrived on the scene! This is much more than too little too late. Egregiously, regardless of any show of force through their massive PR machine, the online facts do not support said volte-face. Effectively, they can hire a football stadium full of experts to scope out militant Islamic jihadists, but that is a far cry from actually bringing them to heel.

What springs to mind is Wilf Hey's well-known quote, "Garbage in, garbage out."[13] So in the same manner in which a qualified police force is tasked - for whatever political reason - to perform like keystone cops by *standing down*, similarly, Facebook's newly developed counterterror squads are instructed to comport themselves. In reality, no amount of coaxing would ever persuade Facebook's hierarchy to admit as much. Nonetheless, the inherent proofs substantiated within this book can't be wished away. Smoked.

Besides, if Facebook was actually doing their best to keep Islamic terrorists (and supporters) off the site, the grade they should be given for their efforts is a resounding "F". No ifs, ands, or buts. Clearly, Facebook needs to stick to what it was originally set up for, an online forum for discussion, and leave the serious work of counterterrorism to true professionals who take their work seriously.

That brings us to the third part of our discussion, providing real solutions to the Facebook problem. By now it should be obvious that the social media giant needs to be dragged, kicking and screaming if necessary, out of its Twilight Zone existence and back to this place we like to call reality.

PART III – HOW TO FIX THE PROBLEMS AND THE OBSTACLES THAT MUST BE OVERCOME

CHAPTER EIGHT

LEGAL OBSTACLES
AND POSSIBLE SOLUTIONS

While Americans hardly back away from filing lawsuits, particularly when believing that a wrong has been committed, the fact remains that the United States is not the most litigious country, as often opined. This will likely come as news to many, in so far as Americans have a reputation for "suing at the drop of a hat". That being said, as indicated below, the United States falls right in the middle of the top ten most "lawsuit happy" nations, coming in at a solid number five. It is a middling position, to be certain. According to *doeLegal Journal*, the following is more than noteworthy:

> . . . *In his book "Exploring Global Landscapes of Litigation", (Baden-Banen: Nomos, 1998), Christian Wollschlager notes that the litigation rates per 1,000 people shows that the US is well down the list of the world's most litigious countries. Without having read the book I refer second to the fact that in his draft testimony before the House Committee on the Judiciary of June, 20, 2004, Theodore Eisenberg, Henry Allen Mark Professor of Law at Cornell University includes Wollschlager's data and relies heavily on it. In that study, Wollschlager found the following:*

Country cases per one thousand population

- *Germany 123.2*

- *Sweden 111.2*

- *Israel 96.8*

- *Austria 95.9*

- *U.S.A. 74.5*

- *UK/England & Wales 64.4*

- *Denmark 62.5*

- *Hungary 52.4*

- *Portugal 40.7*

- *France 40.3* [1]

In this regard, it has already been noted in the introduction:

> *"With over 1.6 billion users worldwide, Facebook is clearly the largest social media site on the planet. For all practical purposes, Facebook has become the de facto Internet since nearly every site connects to it in one form or another. With that size comes great power -- the power to lift up and the power to destroy. CEO Mark Zuckerberg has been caught on an open microphone promising to stifle negative stories of "migrants" and he recently promised the world's Muslims to make his site an open and welcoming place for them.*
>
> *But as we will illustrate, the company has already been doing that. In the process, it has falsely accused many users, banning them from certain features on the flimsiest of contrived "evidence," and has torn down pages over patently false claims and claims*

that are questionable at best. Many of these actions have caused financial losses, but it seems America's legal profession has been cowed into acquiescence by the company's sheer size.

We frequently hear politicians speak of companies not being too big to fail. But is Facebook too big to be regulated? Is Facebook so big that it can freely operate as a government unto itself?" Indeed.

In reality, to seek even a modicum of legal relief against Facebook, this book has amply documented that mega obstacles stand in the way. The hurdles fall into two main quagmire-like arenas: Facebook's behemoth size and its nexus to world leaders. Essentially, what comes to mind is the saying, "you can't fight city hall" on steroids!

To wit, it was not unexpected to find out that (more than) a few of the most hard-charging litigation firms in the United Stated declined to file lawsuits against Facebook, even when presented with legitimate causes of action for legal redress.

On the other hand, there exists a paltry number of litigation specialists (specifically, within public interest firms) who are willing to take on the mantle for the betterment of all, as they battle against monster-size entities. One such exception is Larry Klayman. According to Wikipedia, "Klayman is a politically conservative American public interest lawyer and former Justice Department attorney who has been called a 'Clinton nemesis' for his dozens of lawsuits against the Bill Clinton administration in the 90s. The founder of Judicial Watch and the government watchdog group Freedom Watch, he has brought legal action against former Vice President Dick Cheney, President Barack Obama, OPEC, Iranian President Mahmoud Ahmadinejad, Supreme Court Justice Elena Kagan, Facebook CEO Mark Zuckerberg, and the National Security Agency (NSA). In the last case, a federal judge ruled in December 2013 that the NSA's bulk collection of telephony metadata violated the Fourth Amendment." [2]

Back in April 2011, he filed a lawsuit against Facebook and Zuckerberg in the Superior Court of the District of Columbia

Civil Division for one billion dollars.[3] As is par for the course, a final decision was handed down in June 2014 in favor of Facebook: United States Court of Appeals For The District Of Colombia Circuit argued February 25, 2014 and decided June 13, 2014. It held, in part:

> *The district court held that the Communications Decency Act of 1996, 47 U.S.C. § 230, shielded Zuckerberg and Facebook from suit. We affirm. In enacting the Communications Decency Act, Congress found that the Internet and related computer services "offer a forum for a true diversity of political discourse, unique opportunities for cultural development, and myriad avenues for intellectual activity." 47 U.S.C. § 230(a). The Internet has done so, Congress stressed, "with a minimum of government regulation." Id. Congress accordingly made it the "policy of the United States" to "promote the continued development of the Internet," and "to preserve the vibrant and competitive free market that presently exists for the Internet and other interactive computer services, unfettered by Federal or State regulation[.]" Id. § 230(b). To that end, Section 230(c) of the Act commands that "[n]o provider or user of an interactive computer service shall be treated as the publisher or speaker of any information provided by another information content provider." 47 U.S.C. § 230(c)(1). A later section of the Act adds preemptive bite to that prohibition, providing that "[n]o cause of action may be brought and no liability may be imposed under any State or 3 local law that is inconsistent with this section." Id. § 230(e)(3). As relevant here, the Act defines a protected "interactive computer service" as "any information service, system, or access software provider that provides or enables computer access by multiple users to a computer server, including specifically a service or system that provides access to the Internet[.]" 47 U.S.C. § 230(f)(2). An information content provider, in turn, is defined as "any person or entity that is responsible, in whole or in part, for the creation*

or development of information provided through the Internet or any other interactive computer service." Id. § 230(f)(3)[4]

In layman's terms, the ruling is broken down into several components, all of which shield Facebook (and other internet entities) from accountability. Effectively, under the twenty-year-old Communications Decency Act of 1996, 47 U.S.C. § 230, Facebook meets the standards set out there-under. Thereby, it can operate sans a minimum of government oversight, completely unfettered. Furthermore, the Court held, under the policy of the U.S. as represented by Congress, it must provide an environment free of Federal and State regulations and restraints.

As such, Facebook cannot be held legally liable as a regular publisher can, or as a speaker for anyone who provides content thereof. More specifically, the Act precludes any cause of action which is inconsistent with its overall basis. What it boils down to is this: essentially, those who create or develop any part of the Internet, as a service provider or a system, are protected from legal measures.

And this is precisely why Congress must revisit the aforementioned two-decades old Act. As a matter of record, it was conceived eight years before Facebook exploded onto the scene in February 2004. So even though Islam's soldiers have been operational for centuries, yes, you read that right, it wasn't until Facebook opened its internet door to them that a force multiplier emerged. What this means is patently and painfully obvious: conclusively, what was appropriate in 1996 can no longer stand as is, and on its own merits. It is that simple and that clear.

Incidentally, this section of the law is now the subject of a lawsuit brought against Attorney General Loretta Lynch on behalf of Pam Geller, Robert Spencer, and their respective websites. According to the lawsuit, this section of the Communications Decency Act essentially allows for government-sanctioned censorship.[5]

The core questions become: Is Facebook really "offering a forum for a true diversity of political discourse . . ." in as much as we have proven that its nebulous community standards are, in fact, double standards? Moreover, does Facebook live up to the absolute intent of the Communications Decency Act of 1996, 47 U.S.C.§ 230 by opening up opportunities for cultural development, and myriad avenues for intellectual activities? Intrinsically, is militant jihad now considered within the bounds of cultural and intellectual activities? Is it the considered opinion of the court(s) that lending a "home" to militant jihadists who plot the slaughter of infidels the world over, with Jews, Christians, and other minorities as their targets, meets the rigorous standards of the aforementioned Congressional Act, let alone passes the smell test?

Clearly, as mentioned, the legal obstacles are Herculean. Still yet, there is a silver lining. As highlighted within these pages, a proven fighter within Israel's legal arena, Shurat HaDin (Israel Law Center), has taken on Facebook. Its basis is filed under Lakin v. Facebook.

On October 26, 2015, Shurat HaDin-Israel Law Center, filed an unprecedented lawsuit against Facebook on behalf of some 20,000 Israelis to stop allowing Palestinian terrorists to incite violent attacks against Israeli citizens and Jews on its internet platform. The Complaint seeks an injunction against Facebook requiring it to monitor incitement and to respond immediately to complaints about inciting content.

The Complaint was filed in response to a wave of terror attacks beginning in October 2015 by which Palestinians attacked people with knives, axes, screwdrivers, cars and Molotov cocktails for no reason other than a perception by the attacker that the victims are Jewish. Many of these attackers were motivated to commit their heinous crimes by incitement to murder and the glorification of violence against innocent civilians they read on Facebook. 76 year old Richard Lakin, the lead plaintiff in the case, was brutally attacked by two such Palestinian terrorists, as he rode Bus 78 in Jerusalem's Armon HaNatziv neighborhood on October 13, 2015. He was left with life threatening injuries after being shot in the head and stabbed in the stomach and died of his wounds two weeks later. The 20,000 Israelis that joined the lawsuit all live in fear of their personal safety and security as a result of this violent incitement and want to see Facebook change its policies.

The Complaint alleges that Facebook is much more than neutral internet platform or a mere "publisher" of speech because its algorithms connect the terrorists to the inciters. Facebook actively assists the inciters to find people who are interested in acting on their hateful messages by offering friend, group and event suggestions and targeting advertising based on people's online "likes" and internet browsing history. Additionally, Facebook often refuses to take down the inciting pages, claiming that they do not violate its "community standards." Calling on people to commit crimes is not constitutionally protected speech and endangers the lives of Jews and Israelis. Shurat HaDin will pursue the claims against Facebook on behalf of its 20,0000 clients until Facebook . . . will not allow itself to serve as a tool for terrorists to transmit their rabble rousing messages to their followers and that incitement to anti-Semitic violence will not be tolerated on its website.[6]

And for further edification as to the whys and wherefores regarding the necessity of said lawsuits, consider the story of a mother of six who was murdered when an Arab terrorist broke into her home.[7]

As the reader has come to realize and recognize, Facebook is the de facto gathering place for incitement to jihad. And little excites militant Islamic jihadists like the killing of Jews, and the concomitant preparations thereof. As always, Israel bears the brunt of their fervor and furor.

In this regard, take the case of one (out of countless) murderous rampage, this time in Otniel. It is a town in the southern Har

Hevron region of Judea, Judaism's cradle within Israel. In January 2016, Dafna Meir, a 39-year-old nurse, a mother to six children, two of them foster children, was slaughtered by an Arab terrorist who broke into her home. Despite being stabbed repeatedly, she fought valiantly for her life, while struggling to protect her children. Tragically, she succumbed to her wounds, leaving behind six orphans and a much bereaved husband.

In no uncertain terms, as amply exhibited in this book, Facebook bears a particular onus for providing a *safe* place for barbarians steeped in nihilistic Islam. No doubt, the site has become an enabler in every sense of the word.

Sadly, incidents like this happen far too often.

Significantly, Shurat HaDin has highly notable wins under its belt. In November 2014, for example, it won a landmark decision against the Palestinian Authority. Accordingly, due to the evidence presented by Shurat HaDin:

> *"The United States District Court for the Southern District of New York has ruled that the families of eleven American terrorist victims can proceed to trial against the Palestinian Authority (PA) and the Palestine Liberation Organization (PLO). The families' civil lawsuit, originally brought in 2004, will be tried in January 2015, according to the Court. In a 23-page ruling, the Court rejected the defendants' request to have the case dismissed, finding that there was sufficient evidence to present to a jury concerning the PA and PLO's provision of material support and resources for seven separate attacks in Israel that killed and injured the American citizens. The court also found that the jury could hold the PA vicariously liable on six of the seven attacks."* [8]

Not only that, in 2008, Shurat HaDin brought a civil action lawsuit against the government of North Korea and won! In point of fact, they are front-line fighters for those directly affected by militant jihadists *a la* their campaigns of worldwide terror, whether the victims are Jewish or not.

In January 2000, North Korean agents kidnapped Reverend Kim Dong Shik, a permanent resident of the U.S., from his missionary work assisting North Korean refugees in China. Reverend Kim was then placed in a detention camp in North Korea and was subsequently tortured until his death.

Pursuant to the official policy of North Korea prior to and leading up to Reverend Kim Dong Shik's abduction, torture and murder, North Korea's official security services actively hunted down and abducted refugees and defectors who had crossed into China, as well as other perceived enemies of the regime, and brought these abductees to North Korea where they were imprisoned, tortured and frequently murdered. Reverend Kim had relocated to China in 1993 to provide humanitarian and religious services to the families of North Korean defectors and refugees who had fled across the Sino-Korean border in search of asylum. The North Korean security service, upon learning of Reverend Kim's activities on behalf of the defectors and refugees, abducted and forcibly transferred him to a labor camp in North Korea to thwart his work on behalf of those who had escaped.

In November 2009, Reverend Kim's family filed suit against North Korea under the Foreign Sovereign Immunities Act (FSIA) in the D.C. District Court for their activities in connection with Reverend Kim's abduction and torture. Plaintiffs secured an entry of default against North Korea but were denied default judgment for failure to meet the high standard set for proof of torture under FSIA.

In December 2014, the U.S. Court of Appeals for the District of Columbia reversed the District Court's decision, ruling that the plaintiffs provided enough evidence to hold North Korea liable for Kim's torture and suspected killing. The case was sent back to the lower court for a default judgment in favor of Kim's family.

In April 2015, the DC federal court granted the plaintiffs a historic $330 million default award judgment against the government of North Korea in a civil damages trial for wrongful death, torture and kidnapping.[9]

Incontestably, to have Shurat HaDin's legal eagles in one's corner, well, it is not an overstatement to suggest that overcoming the aforementioned Herculean obstacles are not out of reach.

Along this same volatile terrain, Larry Klayman - though unsuccessful against Facebook in his personal lawsuit - more than hit the mark in stopping Zuckerberg's 'Terrorism Network', his September 2014 article at World Net Daily. Bull's-eye.

Not one to mince words, he accurately coined Mark Zuckerberg's unethical climb to the top of the financial heap, as well as laid bare the platform's inextricable linkage to a myriad of militant jihadi terror groups. There is no doubt about this. Bullet proof.

As depicted in the movie "The Social Network," Zuckerberg infamously stepped on the toes of the very people who helped him rise to the top for his own financial gain. For example, Zuckerberg settled with the "Winklevoss twins" after they sued Zuckerberg for ripping off their idea to program a social networking site they had founded called ConnectU, before Zuckerberg launched Facebook. In another example, Zuckerberg outlined in an email his plan to dilute co-founder Eduardo Savarin's shares down from more than 30 percent without modifying the stakes that were held by other shareholders. (See "6 People Mark Zuckerberg burned on his way to the top" by Courtney Palis, Huffington Post, May 17, 2012.) This sort of "toe-stepping" is only the beginning and hardly a taste of Zuckerberg's less-than-credible, money-hungry reputation. My next example is far more serious.

Due to the lack of liability attached to Internet entities, such as Facebook, for permitting and furthering terrorist conduct on their forums, terrorists groups are using the network to grow much stronger. As outlined in my lawsuit against Facebook and Zuckerberg, I came across the "Third Intifada Page" on Facebook. The page, which had over 300,000 followers, contained terrorist death threats and calls to carry out said death threats against all Jews. As a person of Jewish origin and pro-Israel activist with a highly public opposition to radical Islam, I feared an imminent attack to cause me severe bodily harm or even death. My fears were justified because I received death threats as a result of the page. Consequently, I, along with the public diplomacy minister of Israel, simply asked Facebook to take down the page. Facebook refused, and as a result, Jews actually DIED. The page remained on Facebook for a staggering two weeks! ^10

As a result, it is the considered opinion of this book's co-authors that a forerunner solution to the legal obstacle(s) rests within a particular approach, one which has a proven track record in lawsuits against gargantuan entities: class action suits. And while this is not the address to discuss the ins and outs of how to choose the most adept legal counsel for the (public interest) task at hand, the above stated facts stand on their own merits.

Even so, it is not the only tactical method. Intrinsically, an increasing number of individuals who operate in the public domain (outside the bubble in which leftists congregate and mirror one another) are questioning the double standards invoked by social media in general and by Facebook in particular. Specifically, akin to much of the evidence presented in this book, an aggregate of similar experiences can no longer be dismissed as anecdotal, but must be viewed as fact-based.

This exact issue was raised at a White House press conference on March 4, 2016, eliciting proof of the same via actual "advice" to "open a legal door." On that day, Milo Yiannopoulos, tech editor for Breitbart News, confronted White House Press Secretary Josh Earnest about the censorship many conservatives face on social media sites like Facebook and Twitter. When asked what mechanisms are in place for conservatives who believe they have been unfairly targeted by these sites, Earnest said he wasn't certain what the government could do, but suggested using the courts.

"They're supposed to be insulated from politics, they're supposed to be in a position to resolve those kinds of questions," he said. "So if there are private citizens who believe their constitutional rights are being violated in some way, they do have an opportunity to address that before a judge in a court of law . . . But even that is predicated on the idea that our court system is insulated from partisan politics."[11]

Conclusively, a groundbreaking legal case can be made that Facebook is practicing a form of viewpoint discrimination, through the enforcement of a series of policies invoking double standards, against those with whom they disagree politically and ideologically. Pointedly, silencing those raising their voices against the absorption of millions of Islamic "migrants" (better known in the Islamic world as a Qur'an mandated hijrah . . . migration for the Cause of Allah) into the west smacks of harassment and a blatant violation of their rights. [12]

Consequentially, it is through their own apparent policies of discrimination against viewpoints contrary to their own that a volume of evidence is accumulating, and at an exponential rate. Hence, Facebook invariably steps into the basic First Amendment arena of the right to self-expression, and can no longer hide behind its own political and ideological bent by claiming "incitement" against their preferred "protected" group(s). Besides, it is hard to imagine that an unbiased jury would conclude that a tidal wave of militant jihadists engulfing the west require protection from those whose only "crime" is to raise their voices via free-expression on social media! Concomitantly, any exposure to all the attendant legal costs and burdens should be considered a direct outgrowth of Facebook's own seemingly discriminatory actions.

As a result, the overriding questions before the reader become: Will *larger than life* western-based companies be allowed to shield themselves from discriminatory policies and practices without bearing the financial consequences of their provable actions? And if a clear bias is found against conservatives, for whatever views they hold, be they social, religious or political in nature, will the hammer blow of the courts come down as quickly as they do against companies, for example, who merely refuse to bake a wedding cake for same-sex couples? [13]

Demonstrably, while court-ordered monetary relief against companies (from teeny tiny ones to those larger in size) is a real threat against those whose religious beliefs jut up against prevailing PC dictates, by demanding that they perform certain services or be fined, others, be they public or private entities, have rights which are held as sacrosanct. Effectively, will the Constitutional right to self-expression (with knock-on blows to religious freedom) be relegated to little more than a footnote in American history? Is this (now) the American way?

Moreover, two significant follow-on questions loom overhead: In America, are one's rights only protected when they coincide with the worldview of leaders (elected and non-elected elitists) who are in a position to make the rules according to their ideological persuasion, the Constitution be damned? Even more so, is this the case when they operate publicly-held companies which are (in more ways than one) akin to governments onto themselves?

Trenchantly, it is not a question of whether or not lawsuits should be lodged against Facebook. In reality, its necessity has already been proven. That ship has sailed. Rather, Sun Tzu style pro-active measures should be given the utmost consideration and focus for westerners, who are rightfully frightened about the tailwind given to militant jihadists. Therefore, think: tactical and strategic imperatives are needed to stop Facebook's *terrorism network*.

Onward and upward. From strength to strength. As is said in Israel: Kadima!

CHAPTER NINE

POSSIBLE POLITICAL SOLUTIONS AND OBSTACLES

I t should be obvious by now that Facebook is unlikely to implement any positive changes on its own. It's also clear that Facebook, and other social media sites, need oversight from a bipartisan group of elected officials.

Consider that Facebook's CEO has the ear of heads of state, like German Chancellor Angela Merkel and Chinese President Xi Jinping. Additionally, his company has a firm grip on elected members of Congress, if one considers the amount of money the company gives to office holders. Moreover, Zuckerberg is becoming more political with each passing day, advocating far-left policies on issues like immigration.

By the end of February 2016, the Facebook Inc. Political Action Committee had given over $300,000 to candidates from both parties. Democrats received 46 percent of those contributions while Republican candidates received 54 percent of the donations.[1] In 2014, the company gave $375,500 to federal candidates, with Republicans receiving 51 percent of those donations.[2]

Of course, Facebook has the right to participate in the political process, but one has to wonder if the recipients of those monies would be willing to support legislation designed to rein in overbearing social media sites.

Speaking of the political process and Facebook's "revolving door" access to Congress and President Obama, *The Hill*, a more than reputable news outlet, reporting on the comings and goings within the Beltway, wrote on April 22, 2016:

Facebook founder Mark Zuckerberg has increasingly used his perch atop his massive social media platform to speak out on political issues — including immigration reform, the Syrian refugee crisis, and solidarity with the Muslim community.

While Zuckerberg's veiled shot last week at Donald Trump's call for a wall on the Mexican border was a rare entry into the presidential debate, the Facebook creator has regularly made his views known on debates of the day.

Zuckerberg and Facebook have an enormous influence over the political debate because of their business, which is used by the candidates and their supporters as a messaging and recruiting tool to deliver and share news about their campaigns.

The confluence of events will put Zuckerberg and Facebook in the spotlight, especially when he chooses to makes his views known.

"It is no surprise that tech CEOs are trying to use their platform to influence political change and that they may be quite trusted, given the low amount of trust that people feel toward politicians as a broader group," said Margie Omero, who leads research at the firm Purple Strategies. "That said people have more interaction with the product than they do with the CEO."

Zuckerberg himself called his lofty speech last week at a developers conference unlike any he had given.

Aside from previewing Facebook's 10-year roadmap, he also used the speech to challenge people to choose "hope over fear" and criticized "fearful voices calling for building walls" — a phrase many interpreted as a knock at Trump.

Though the company recently tried to pour cold water on the idea that Facebook would ever use its product to try to skim support from any candidate, a spokeswoman said Zuckerberg would continue to speak out on public policy.

"Facebook's mission is to connect the world and bring people together – Mark will continue to advocate for public policies to the extent that it helps advance our mission or the mission of the Chan Zuckerberg Initiative," a Facebook spokeswoman said, referring to the charitable company led by the company's founder and his wife, Priscilla Chan.

Just in the last several months, Zuckerberg has spoken out on a number of hotly debated issues, including a handful apparently aimed at Trump.

In December, Zuckerberg shared a post that was liked 1.5 million times assuring the Muslim community that they were "always welcome" on Facebook. His words came a day after Trump had called for a complete ban on Muslims entering the United States.

Zuckerberg has been most active on the issue of immigration reform in recent years, helping to found an advocacy group FWD. us to push reform and using one of his few visits to Washington back in 2013 to lobby on the issue.

It made sense that Zuckerberg's most biting line during last week's speech was widely interpreted as a repudiation of Trump's position to finish building a wall along the U.S.-Mexico border to cut off the flow of immigrants illegally entering the country.

"I don't pretend that our press releases get the same attention as when Mark speaks out on this issue by any means," FWD. us president Todd Schulte said, adding that he is "thankful and proud" to have a founder so dedicated to the issue.

Zuckerberg has been testing out a milder version of the "building walls" line for months now.

"As I travel around the world, I see many nations turning inwards. I hear growing voices for building walls and distancing people labeled as 'other,'" Zuckerberg wrote early last month after signing an amicus brief to the Supreme Court to support President Obama's executive action on immigration.

Some advocates who are strongly opposed to Trump applauded Zuckerberg's words but have already called for follow through — specifically to publicly vow that Facebook will not participate in the Republican convention this year. Groups like ColorOfChange have been putting pressure on other major companies like Google, Microsoft and Coca-Cola to pull their sponsorship.

"With comments like those made by Mark Zuckerberg, it is our hope that he and others will show the same level of integrity when it comes to rejecting the violent rhetoric and policies being espoused by Donald Trump by refusing to invest in the RNC Convention," said Rashad Robinson, who leads ColorOfChange.

Facebook is not the specific target of that pressure campaign and the company declined to respond to that question.

On other issues, Zuckerberg has found that circumstances forced him to address dicey political topics including net neutrality in other countries and support for the black lives movement.

Aside from Zuckerberg's speeches and Facebook posts, he has also donated millions to political causes in years past. And Facebook itself, has become a lobbying powerhouse in Washington. . . [3]

Incontestably, this book's unapologetic assertion that Facebook is akin to a government unto itself, desperately in need of reining in, is a vast understatement. And, apparently, some in the (usually somnolent) Senate actually agree! So along comes another knock-on effect from the whistleblower (a blessing on his head), as the Senate Commerce Committee weighed in on May 10, 2016.

The US Senate Commerce Committee—which has jurisdiction over media issues, consumer protection issues, and internet communication—has sent a letter to Mark Zuckerberg requesting answers to questions it has on its trending topics section. The letter comes after Gizmodo on Monday reported on allegations by one former news curator, who worked for Facebook as a contractor, that the curation team routinely suppressed or blacklisted topics of interest to conservatives. That report also included allegations from several former curators that they used a "injection tool" to add or bump stories onto the trending module.

The letter asks that Facebook "arrange for your staff including employees responsible for trending topics to brief committee staff on this issue." The letter was signed by Chairman for the Committee on Commerce, Science, and Transportation, Senator John Thune (R) from South Dakota.

Some of the letter's questions include:

1 *Please describe Facebook's organization structure for the Trending Topics feature, and the steps for determining included topics. Who is ultimately responsible for approving its content?*

2 *Have Facebook news curators in fact manipulated the content of the Trending Topics section, either by targeting news stories related to conservative views for exclusion or by injecting non-trending content?*

3 *What steps is Facebook taking to investigate claims of politically motivated manipulation of news stories in the Trending Topics section? If such claims are substantiated, what steps will Facebook take to hold the responsible individuals accountable?*

4 *In a statement responding to the allegations, Facebook has claimed to have "rigorous guidelines in place for the review team" to prevent "the suppression of political perspectives" or the "prioritization of one viewpoint ver another or one news outlet over another."*

  a *When did Facebook first introduce these guidelines?*

  b *Please provide a copy of these guidelines, as well as any changes or amendments since January 2014.*

c *Does Facebook provide training for its employees related to these guidelines? If so, describe what the training consists of, as well as its frequency.*

d *How does Facebook determine compliance with these guidelines? Does it conduct audits? If so, how often? What steps are taken when a violation occurs?*

5 *Does Facebook maintain a record of curators decisions to inject a story into the Trending Topics section or target a story for removal? If such a record is not maintained, can such decisions be reconstructed or determined based on an analysis of the Trending Topics product?*

a *If so, how many stories have curators excluded that represented conservative viewpoints or topics of interest to conservatives? How many stories did curators inject that were not, in fact, trending?*

b *Please provide a list of all news stories removed from or injected into the Trending Topics section since January 2014 . . .* [4]

To be certain, legislation is the only viable way to rein in Zuckerberg's behemoth and put a stop to his online reign of terror.

Specifically, there are three pieces of legislation that need to be considered, passed, and signed into law. The first would require social media sites to cooperate with authorities involved with counterterrorism. Secondly, Congress needs to immediately pass legislation amending Section 230 of the Communications Decency Act to give online users the right to sue in the event Facebook censors protected speech. The third bill would essentially be a *social media user's bill of rights* that would prevent the kind of abuses we have documented in this book.

The first measure has already been introduced. In December 2015, Sen. Dianne Feinstein, D-California, introduced a measure in the Senate known as S.2372, or the Requiring Reporting of Online Terrorist Activity Act.[5] This isn't the first time it was introduced.

A somewhat different version of this bill was introduced earlier in the year, but was scrapped partly over concerns that it would make sites like Facebook monitor all activity and possibly misidentify individuals as terrorists while violating users' privacy.

The measure simply reads:

> *"Whoever, while engaged in providing an electronic communication service or a remote computing service to the public through a facility or means of interstate or foreign commerce, obtains actual knowledge of any terrorist activity, including the facts or circumstances described in subsection (c), shall, as soon as reasonably possible, provide to the appropriate authorities the facts or circumstances of the alleged terrorist activities."*

The bill adds:

> *"The facts or circumstances described in this subsection, include any facts or circumstances from which there is an apparent violation of section 842(p) of title 18, United States Code, that involves distribution of information relating to explosives, destructive devices, and weapons of mass destruction."*[6]

The measure also precludes monitoring, so Internet privacy is theoretically preserved.

The proposal has only attracted three co-sponsors, including Feinstein and her Republican counterpart on the committee. One other Democrat has signed on to the measure, and it is currently collecting dust in the Senate Judiciary Committee.

We reached out to lawmakers but have so far received no response.

Why has there been no action on the measure? There are a few possible reasons.

It could be that 2016 is an election year, and politicians want to keep the money flowing from companies like Facebook. Second, there are very legitimate concerns that the measure could be used against innocent American citizens who happen to identify with a political ideology the administration disagrees with.

That is hardly a stretch of the imagination. In 2011, for example, Vice President Joe Biden accused Tea Party Republicans of acting like terrorists, and a 2013 Rasmussen poll found that one in four voters who support Barack Obama believe the Tea Party is the greatest terror threat to the United States. "Among those who Strongly Approve of the president more fear the tea party than radical Muslims," the report said.

In 2013, the IRS revealed that it had targeted conservative groups, including some Tea Party organizations that had applied for tax-exempt status. That scandal still has not been fully resolved, even though the Justice Department had a "powerful case" against the agency.[7] It would not be a stretch for a future administration to declare certain groups "terrorists" in an effort to clamp down on dissent. If Feinstein's measure becomes law, it could be used against US citizens with an opposing point of view.

There is another, even more horrifying, possible reason the measure has not been considered. For years, concerns have been raised that organizations like the Muslim Brotherhood have become firmly entrenched in the halls of power. It would not take much for these groups to declare the law *Islamophobic* should it be seriously considered. That, in and of itself, would be more than enough to permanently table the measure in the current political climate.

This brings us to the third proposed measure, since the second has already been addressed. Under the status quo, users of social media have fewer rights than suspects in a criminal trial. Those individuals have the right to due process, the right to examine evidence and witnesses against them, the right to present a defense and the right to appeal if convicted. In short, they are considered innocent until proven guilty beyond a reasonable doubt.

This is not the case with sites like Facebook and Twitter, where one is considered guilty, even if he or she proves their innocence beyond a doubt. Worse yet, most users aren't given a chance to appeal whatever punishment moderators hand out. Users who happen to be somewhat well known, however, often get their situations rectified in fairly short order. This was the case with Jan Morgan, and it was the case when Facebook slapped Fox News' Todd Starnes over a post supportive of the NRA, Paula Deen, and Jesus Christ.[8]

In those situations, Facebook reversed their actions, calling them "mistakes." Average users, for the most part, get no such consideration. They are simply declared guilty and punished, usually with no recourse.

Many argue that Facebook provides a free service to users who are themselves free to use it or not, and as such, Facebook can do pretty much what it wants. There's only one problem with that line of thought. Industries across the United States are routinely regulated by federal and state authorities. Banks, oil companies, and pharmaceutical companies are just a few of the industries that must follow state and federal laws. Why not social media? Facebook, after all, holds a near-monopoly on social media. Companies like AT&T have been broken up for having the kind of monopoly Mark Zuckerberg enjoys.

Speaking at the annual Jerusalem Post Conference in New York in May, Israel's Internal Security Minister Gilad Erdan said social media sites like Facebook need to do more to stop incitement to terrorism. If those sites refuse to take action, he said, governments need to step in.

"I call on Mark Zuckerberg, Larry Page, Sergey Brin and their colleagues to take the initiative to monitor and remove this incitement on their own. If they refuse and continue to ignore their role in promoting incitement, governments must pass legislation forcing them to do so." "Today they are part of the problem," Erdan said. "They must become part of the solution." [9]

But getting government to take action is far easier said than done. Politicians like to pound their chests and call for *common-sense* legislation. Yet when presented with a very real problem, they shy away. This is the point where individuals need to step up and take action.

CHAPTER TEN

WHAT INDIVIDUAL USERS CAN DO ABOUT FACEBOOK

As it turns out, there's quite a bit individuals can do, short of picking up pitchforks and torches and storming Facebook's Menlo Park offices.

LEAVE FACEBOOK

Some have suggested leaving Facebook for good, but with a user base that exceeds 1.6 billion registered users, that is simply not a viable option. Even if 100 million users instantly left Facebook, the problem would remain, it would just affect 100 million fewer people for a short period of time. Many of those users would probably come back to the site, and the numbers would be back up in short order.

REPORT ABUSES AND BANS

One site, OnlineCensorship.org, gives users the opportunity to report censorship by any of the main social media sites, including Facebook. The site says it "seeks to encourage companies to operate with greater transparency and accountability toward their users as they make decisions that regulate speech."

"We know they're big fans of data—so we're collecting reports from their users in an effort to shine a light on what content is taken down, why companies make certain decisions about content, and how content takedowns are affecting communities of users around the world," the site adds on its "About" page. Users can, and should, make use of this site to report instances where content is removed or banned based on false reports.

FACEBOOK ALTERNATIVES

Many have wondered about setting up alternatives to Facebook. Several alternatives have already been set up, but unfortunately, they do not have the reach that Facebook has, and alternative sites do absolutely nothing to solve the problems associated with Facebook.

Consider Tea Party Community, for example. With over 161,000 registered users, the site is one of, if not the, largest alternative on the Internet. While impressive, it simply doesn't even come close to the number of people Facebook reaches. In addition to reach, there are other problems that hinder alternative Facebook-like sites.

In order for any alternative site to have a lasting impact, it would need to be well-funded and well-planned. It's not just enough to create a site using tools like PhpFox. While such sites may work for small, targeted, niche audiences, they cannot begin to compete with Facebook.

First, the cost to build the infrastructure of such a site is well beyond the means of most average users. In order to build a secure, robust platform for such a site, one would have to spend a great deal of money in servers, routers, and other hardware if one uses traditional methods. Add to that the cost of maintaining the equipment in a data center and the cost of IT support to keep it all running, and one can easily spend many thousands of dollars.

Rick Ferran, the owner of Uncle Sam's Misguided Children, for example, said he spent over thirty-thousand dollars on a Facebook alternative. Second, the legal requirements of such sites would also require a fairly significant investment in legal fees and attorney costs. Add to that the fact that any alternative site would be operating in an environment created largely by Facebook, and it's quite unlikely owners of alternative sites would have the ear of elected officials.

Tim Selaty, Sr., the founder of Tea Party Community, said he was able to keep costs down by using a "cloud" strategy working with Amazon. The site is secure and robust and a new server can be set up fairly easily and quickly if needed. Having friends in the legal profession also helped, he added. Nevertheless, his outlay is still around four-thousand dollars per month.

The biggest problem, he explained, is the sheer number of hackers and "trolls" who attack the site on a daily basis. That doesn't mean alternatives shouldn't be established. Competition always improves quality, but those who wish to create an alternative site should be aware of the potential pitfalls and remember that Facebook didn't start as a global mega-site.

LOBBY CONGRESS

As we noted in a previous chapter, legislation has already been introduced to make sites like Facebook report online terror activity to the proper authorities. We also suggested Congress consider taking action to give users protection from the kind of abuses many have experienced and called on lawmakers to amend Section 230 of the Communications Decency Act.

Users need to contact their elected representatives and politely push them to take action on these measures. It may seem like a waste of time, but if enough people make enough noise with enough lawmakers, they will listen. After all, Facebook lobbies Congress, so why shouldn't average users?

Keep in mind that a large number of these officials get campaign contributions from Facebook. These contributions are a matter of public record and can be seen on the website, OpenSecrets.org. Users, especially those who are United States citizens, can and should ask their elected members of Congress why they accept money from a company working to stifle free expression on a global level.

GRASSROOTS ACTIVISM

Users can, of course, protest Facebook's actions both online and in the real world. There have already been a few online protests, with one attracting some thirty-five-thousand users fed up with the site's actions. That protest, known as the Facebook Blackout Day, asked users to temporarily disable their account for a twenty-four hour period.[1]

That protest, started in 2013 by John Vigil, a New Mexico-based physician, caused an uproar by many on the left, who accused organizers and participants of racism. Many participants were banned from Facebook for short periods of time, and the event mysteriously disappeared after Vigil accidentally deactivated his account early.

The protest was also targeted by Facebook, which blocked users from inviting friends to the one-day event. The company also suspended one administrator for writing, "She hasn't nothing to do but come here for attention."[2]

Despite Facebook's best efforts, the protest went off without a hitch. Facebook didn't change its policy enforcement, but the event managed to educate a number of people about the site's abuses. That's not to say protests never work – they do. In 2015, for example, Facebook relaxed a controversial real names policy after a number of drag queens and mostly left-wing rights groups complained.[3]

ECONOMIC PRESSURE

When all is said and done, Facebook is a for-profit company with one primary goal, making money. Facebook doesn't really produce anything one can purchase, but it does provide space for advertising at a cost. Companies that purchase advertising on Facebook can and should be made aware of the site's actions against its users. How many businesses really want to be affiliated with a company that routinely engages in what many see as viewpoint discrimination, or a company that enables jihad?

Granted, many businesses make their decisions based on the bottom line, and advertising on Facebook makes sense. But in doing so, those businesses are actually helping to fund Facebook's actions. This is where individual users can exercise what Adam Smith called the *invisible hand*.[4]

BECOME WISE FACEBOOK USERS

When using a site like Facebook, it's not enough to just know how to do certain things. Anyone using the platform should be aware of the possible traps that could get them in trouble and learn how to avoid them.

- **Watch what you post.** Many Facebook users are careful about what they post or what they say when commenting. There are some individuals, however, who tend to push the envelope. This is a bit like poking a hive full of angry bees. At some point, the person doing the poking will get stung. That's not to say anti-jihad posts should never be put up. Far from it. News articles that deal with the issue need to be disseminated, but it's sometimes far too tempting to caption or lead the post with something that will clearly get the user in trouble. In short, users should be, as the saying goes, wise as serpents. We want to inform, but we shouldn't strive to inflame.

- **Check out all friend requests.** Believe it or not, there are people who send friend requests for the sole purpose of ultimately reporting the user so he or she can get banned. It's quite tempting to accept a friend request, but doing so without first vetting the person can cause untold problems. Check out the person's timeline, especially if you've never heard of him or her. Find out where the person lives and who they claim to work for. If the individual claims to work for Facebook and live in

Morocco, for example, you may want to consider that a major red flag. Ask yourself the following:

How many friends does the person have and who are they? Check out a few of those individuals to see what they have posted.

How many of those are mutual friends? Do you interact with any of them, and what has that experience been like?

How long has the person been on Facebook?

How many posts can you see on his or her timeline? Depending on the privacy settings, you may not see much at all. Some like to display only a few pictures that really don't give you much information about the person. If that's the case, you may want to consider ignoring the friend request.

What kind of posts do you see on the person's timeline? If you can't translate them or if you wholeheartedly disagree with the posts, you may want to consider passing on that request.

Do not, under any circumstances, reach out to the person unless you are fairly confident that individual is legitimate.

- **Block certain countries from accessing your page.** If you own or manage a page on Facebook, you can mitigate a certain amount of trouble by simply blocking or restricting various countries from accessing your page. If you administer a page that is critical of militant jihad, for example, you should probably block majority Muslim countries.

- **Consult with online security specialists.** If you run a page on Facebook, you may want to consult with someone who specializes in Facebook security to ensure your page is configured properly.

- **Document everything.** It's extremely important to document any interaction with Facebook. Most people simply click through the notifications they receive from the site, without taking a few seconds to grab a screenshot. Use something like the Windows Snipping Tool to create an image of what you receive and save it in a safe place, preferably on an external device like a USB drive. Likewise, make sure you archive any emails you receive from the site.

The bottom line is that you, the individual Facebook user, are the single greatest asset in the effort to change Facebook.

CONCLUSION

To paraphrase Apollo 13 astronaut Jim Lovell; Menlo Park, we have a problem. What started as a way to collect information on college students has grown and morphed into a global behemoth that now controls what news is read and threatens to control every aspect of its users' Internet experience.

For those who are somewhat right of center, Facebook has become what Breitbart.com called the "world's most dangerous censor,"[1] silencing those who hold opinions that run contrary to the site's monitors.

As we have documented in the previous chapters, CEO Mark Zuckerberg not only rubs elbows with world leaders like German Chancellor Angela Merkel, he has been caught making promises to stifle certain stories. As a result of an investigation following that promise, Facebook is now on a quest to rid the European continent of speech it deems *hateful*.

This comes at a time when the continent is being overrun by migrants, potentially changing the face of Europe for many decades to come. Sweden, for example, has become what the *Washington Weekly News* called "The Rape Capital of Europe" because there is no punishment for Muslim immigrants who commit rape.[2]

Facebook's response, as we noted earlier, is to punish those who stand with the victims of those sexual assaults. It is along this twisted and frightening path that multicultural devotees reveal their inner psychosis through what amounts to a mental illness gripping many westerners afflicted with this warped, confused, and mentally besieged mindset.

Imagine, if you dare, literally laying out the welcome mat for *refugees* whose fellow militant jihadists have been known to rape, pillage, and otherwise wreak havoc across your country, with other nations in tow, only to invite said related grouping of *guests* to a shindig of sorts, but this time with the expectation of *good* behavior! Pray tell, who are the crazies?

Albert Einstein is credited with saying, "The definition of insanity is doing the same thing over and over again, but expecting different results."[3] Conversely, isn't it also rational and logical to assess the mental sanity of officials who behave counter-intuitive to normal parameters? For isn't it abnormal to organize fantasy-driven gatherings for militant Islamic jihadists who commit rape, with the expectation of *good* behavior? Even more so, what about party officiants who insist on labeling said violations of civilized norms as *incidents*? In all honestly, aren't such fantasists oozing with mental illness? If not, why not?

Shunting aside all the gobbledygook and so-called *humanitarian* ethos, this is where the rubber meets the road. The very fact that the man whose site has "more users than the country of India has residents" believes that "everyone deserves to be connected" attests to his unwillingness (or his inability) to separate those who are civilized from those who are not.[4]

The recent Trending Topics controversy also reveals what happens when one entity holds a near-monopoly on what news is fit to be read. As we've documented, Facebook has stifled certain stories using a number of means, including falsely flagging them as *unsafe*.

Those who openly oppose the concept of militant jihad are often the target of harassment and abusive behavior by site moderators who seem to have no problem making or accepting false reports. As a result, average users have been slapped for reasons that are specious at best, if not downright fabricated. In fact, at times, they are libelous.

Pages and groups that oppose jihad have also been subjected to abusive treatment, and have been unpublished for any reason or no reason at all. In some cases, the site has pulled pages over false claims of nudity, giving page owners very little recourse. Meanwhile, those who do support jihad seem to be given near carte blanche to do whatever they want, even though their actions clearly violate Facebook's standards and in some cases, violate the law. As we documented, some of those individuals have used the site to communicate death threats to those with an opposing point of view. In many cases, Facebook refused to deal with the threats, taking no action against those who issued them.

As Shurat HaDin proved with its video, Facebook moderators have demonstrated a clear bias in favor of Palestinian pages that attack Israel and Jews in general. Although Facebook eventually took the proper action, it did so only after more than a million people watched the NGO's video.

In a concluding nutshell, the left's inviolate belief in multiculturalism and all its permutations thereof has become one of the chief weapons of militant jihadists, as they catapult and devour western civilization at breakneck speed. The examples presented in this book are by no means exhaustive, but they show a very clear and disturbing trend.

Sadly, even when overwhelming evidence of abuse and bias is made known, many in positions of authority refuse to take action. Judges will issue rulings and politicians will thump their chests all the while feathering their campaigns with Zuckerberg's money.

Personalities like Glenn Beck will turn a blind eye and pretend incidents like these didn't really happen. Instead, they choose to look long and lovingly into Zuckerberg's eyes while telling us everything's just fine.

After all, these aren't the droids you're looking for, even though Facebook recently admitted that *rogue employees* may have engaged in ". . .isolated improper actions." [5]

As we noted in the final chapter, the real power rests with the individual. That's right, you the reader, the individual Facebook user.

With the information we've provided you can be a wiser consumer of the social media site. Additionally, you have the power to lobby your representatives in Congress to take the proper action.

After all, Facebook is nothing without you, the individual user.

Buried in the small town of Quanah, Texas, is William Jesse McDonald, a Captain of Texas Rangers known as "a man who would charge hell with a bucket of water." Engraved on his tombstone is this: "No man in the wrong can stand up against a fellow that's in the right and keeps on a-comin'."[6]

Imagine the change that could happen if a majority of Facebook's 1.6 billion registered users were to adopt that philosophy. The alternative is far too horrible to imagine, as Facebook now seeks to essentially control the Internet. If you think things are bad now, just wait five or ten years. Shiver the west's timbers.

JIHAD IN ORLANDO: FACEBOOK TAKES CENTER STAGE

As night follows day, it was hardly unexpected to learn that another militant Islamic jihad attack exploded within America. If it hadn't happened, that would have been the shocker.

But what took many by surprise was the body count in Orlando's Pulse gay nightclub, plus the number of innocents left maimed and permanently scarred for life both physically and emotionally.

And it is into devastating wreckage, the deadliest frontal jihad since September 11, 2001, that all the central players performed on cue. Mind you, no one with functioning brain cells expected President Obama, an avowed Marxist and Islamist, to place the onus squarely where it belonged, thus, uttering three judicious words: radical Islamic terror! What's so hard about that? Sheesh.

Still yet, to be more exact, the main thrust behind **Omar Mir Seddique Mateen's** jihadi slaughter is Islam and its inextricable relationship to blood. Laced with underlying nihilistic tendencies, the Qur'an's madman, Muhammad, dictates all the bloodletting. Let's not pussyfoot around. After all, countless lives hang in the balance. In reality, while the victims this time were gays, rest assured, all infidels, be they Jews, Christians, and every non-Muslim minority in between, are in their cross hairs. Full stop.

As anticipated, the leftward and Islamic captured media went into hyper-drive, yarn-like, they spun what has become incessant fairy tale *reporting*. They parroted Obama's basic mantra: it's the guns, stupid! And as if reading from the same demented script, the troika, namely, Obama Inc., media mouthpieces, and a plethora of smug professorial types, all chimed in with nary a hint about Islam's poisonous roots threatening to upend America. How can this be?

But it gets worse. The Feds possessed overwhelming evidence, relative to Omar Mir Seddique Mateen's jihadi leanings, still yet, what did they do? They let him off the hook! Why would they do that?

In 2014, the FBI hauled him in again over a connection with Moner Mohammad Abu-Salha, a twenty-two-year old Palestinian American. They had grown up together in the small Florida coastal town of Fort Pierce. Abu Salha went off to Syria, joined the al Qaeda-linked Nusra Front and killed himself in a suicide attack by driving a massive truck bomb into a restaurant filled with Syrian government soldiers. Yet the FBI closed the file on Mateen after determining that the links between the two young Muslims did not warrant further inquiry. Compiling all the known data on the Orlando killer with the results of the FBI interviews with him would have placed him high on the list of suspects and called in for further questioning.

The oversights of United States law enforcement, intelligence, and security agencies recur each time Islamist terrorists strike. The Ramadan 2016 attack in Orlando showed that no lessons had been learned from the lapses that led to September 11, 2001.

The FBI erred gravely in closing the case over the Mateen connection with the Palestinian American suicide bomber. This explains why senior FBI officials are downplaying the importance of that connection. When he was exculpated, the federal authorities also discontinued electronic surveillance of the terrorist's movements. So they missed his mounting extremism, his frequent attendance at a mosque led by a radical Imam, who regularly incited his flock to murder ("Gays must die").[1] He thus kept his Security Officer's ID, which gave him access to secure government sites. His name was kept on the list of licensees for carrying firearms.

It is especially hard to understand the lackadaisical handling by federal agents of this prime suspect when FBI Director James Comey reiterated: "The Islamic State remains the top threat America is facing."[2]

Making the security situation exponentially worse, once again, Facebook is smack in the middle of the catastrophic terrain cited above. Par for their course, they lent safe harbor and cover for Orlando's jihadi to freely plot, *friend*, and otherwise engage in preparing his Ramadan *gifts* for Allah! Ain't that sweet, "Ramadan Kareem" to Mark Zuckerberg. Fox News reported:

> *In the hours after he blasted his way into an Orlando gay nightclub, and with his victims lying dead or wounded around him, Omar Mateen took to Facebook to pledge his loyalty to ISIS and threaten more attacks on the civilized world, a key lawmaker privy to the gunman's posts told FoxNews.com Wednesday.*
>
> *Mateen, who killed forty-nine people and wounded fifty-three inside Pulse early Sunday, died when a SWAT team stormed the club. But in the roughly four hours between his initial rampage and his death, the twenty-nine-year-old radicalized Muslim broadcast his twisted message of hate on social media, according to Senate Homeland Security Chairman Ron Johnson, R-Wisconsin.*
>
> *"I pledge my alliance to (ISIS leader) abu bakr al Baghdadi.. may Allah accept me," Mateen wrote in one post early Sunday morning. "The real muslims will never accept the filthy ways of the west" . . . "You kill innocent women and children by doing us airstrikes. now taste the Islamic state vengeance."*
>
> *Mateen's social media accounts were taken down before they could be widely viewed by the public, but Johnson's committee*

investigators have uncovered some or all of them. The senator has also written a letter to Facebook executives expressing concern about Mateen's postings and asking for more information on his activities.

"It is my understanding that Omar Mateen used Facebook before and during the attack to search for and post terrorism-related content," read Johnson's letter. "According to information obtained by my staff, five Facebook accounts were apparently associated with Omar Mateen."3

Ever more ominously, the ante is upped. Concomitantly, the death toll rises. Alas, not to be lost in the increasingly foul stench which surrounds Facebook, hark back to Chapter Seven: Facebook's Counterterror Efforts: Closing the Barn Door After the Horses Have Escaped and recap: "Moreover, from a business perspective, their overall plan to anchor in place teams to monitor this and that makes perfect sense, in anticipation of shielding the company even further, not if, but when class action lawsuits pick up steam."

Similarly, Chapter Eight: Legal Obstacles and Possible Solutions is coming full circle. Yes, recall the advice within: "Clearly, as mentioned, the legal obstacles are Herculean. Still yet, there is a silver lining. As highlighted within these pages, a proven fighter within Israel's legal arena, Shurat HaDin (Israel Law Center), has taken on Facebook. Its basis is filed under *Lakin v Facebook*."

In this regard, it is heartening to find out that a family impacted by Facebook's (and attendant social media giants) refusal to close their platform to militant Islamic jihadists is holding them to (legal) account. Yippee. Of course, it remains to be seen if they prevail. Nevertheless, the fact is that Facebook's enabling is being exposed for what it truly is: unlawful.

The parents of Nohemi Gonzalez, the only American killed in the November 2015 terrorist assault on Paris, have filed a lawsuit against Facebook, Twitter, and Google, which operates YouTube. The federal lawsuit filed at a district court in northern California said the social networks provided *material support* to ISIS that took responsibility for the attack in which 130 people lost their lives.

The parents of the late twenty-three-year-old California student also said in the lawsuit that "Without defendants Twitter, Facebook, and Google (YouTube), the explosive growth of ISIS over the last few years into the most-feared terrorist group in the world would not have been possible."[4] It is still not clear whether the service providers are liable under American law. In response, Twitter and Facebook claimed that the lawsuit is without merit while Google said that it does not comment publicly on pending litigation. The lawsuit is scheduled to be heard in court in September.

But never mind. Wouldn't you know, even after the slaughter-fest in Orlando, Facebook's "community standards" arbiters took action against Pamela Geller, all for daring to point out the obvious. Geller, president of the American Freedom Defense Initiative and author of *The Post-American Presidency: The Obama Administration's War On America*, said Facebook took down her group page, Stop Islamization of America, (then restored it after much back and forth, but who knows for how long) and banned her from posting for thirty days.

The reason? She dared to post about the Islamic terror attack at a gay nightclub in Orlando, Florida.

According to Geller, this was the post that got her in trouble with the speech minders at the social media giant: "The White House fails to mention Islam, jihad or the call for slaughter of gays in Islam. Instead, Obama is importing these savages by the thousands. . . ."[5]

At the same time, according to a conversation this author had with an administrator of "American Bikers United Against Jihad," he was banned for thirty days after posting . . .guess what . . .a picture of Osama bin Laden! Apparently, it also didn't conform to their *stringent*, albeit, nebulous *community standards*. In a never ending vicious cycle, banning and blocking users who are against militant Islamic jihad continues apace at warp speed.

Most significantly, what kind of Orwellian nightmare has America sunk into, whereby the Muslim Brotherhood Mafia and like-minded jihadi groups run amok throughout officialdom and civil society? Meanwhile, the largest Internet platform (housed within California's Silicon Valley) operates as an uncontrollable (publicly held) and unregulated behemoth; the world's most dangerous censor; and a playground for Islam's soldiers for Allah! Incontestably, it is a government unto itself.

Truth dare be told, unless a two-pronged assault plan is immediately executed, America will fall to the sword of Islam. Forthwith, the next administration must clean house to an unprecedented degree, urgently applying the Smith Act (with charges of Sedition) against all Muslim Brotherhood Mafia (Sunni and Shia) front groups.

In tandem, Facebook must be reined in and held to account. Consequentially, not only will America, Israel, and the west be infinitely safer, resultant, the rest of social media's top-tier will fall in line and start acting as responsible corporate citizens. Conclusively, are Americans (westerners at large) to assume that they now have an either/or option: to surrender and submit to Allah, or await their fates, as countless jihadis scream "Allahu Akbar" before they close in for the kill?

Trenchantly, when Zuckerberg promised that Muslims would remain safe and welcome on Facebook, and vowed, "If you're a Muslim in this community, as the leader of Facebook I want you to know that you are always welcome here and that we will fight to protect your rights and create a peaceful and safe environment for you," [6] was he including the likes of Orlando's jihadi?

Sure looks like it.

APPENDIX: EXHIBITS

Exhibit 1. A post falsely attributed to one co-author and formatted to appear as though he created it.

Exhibit 2. A second post falsely attributed to one co-author and formatted to appear as though he created it.

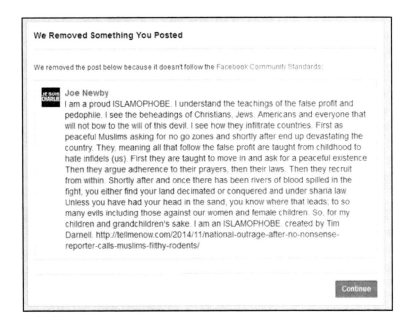

We Removed Something You Posted

We removed the post below because it doesn't follow the Facebook Community Standards:

Joe Newby
I am a proud ISLAMOPHOBE. I understand the teachings of the false profit and pedophile. I see the beheadings of Christians, Jews, Americans and everyone that will not bow to the will of this devil. I see how they infiltrate countries. First as peaceful Muslims asking for no go zones and shortly after end up devastating the country. They, meaning all that follow the false profit are taught from childhood to hate infidels (us). First they are taught to move in and ask for a peaceful existence Then they argue adherence to their prayers, then their laws. Then they recruit from within. Shortly after and once there has been rivers of blood spilled in the fight, you either find your land decimated or conquered and under sharia law. Unless you have had your head in the sand, you know where that leads; to so many evils including those against our women and female children. So, for my children and grandchildren's sake. I am an ISLAMOPHOBE, created by Tim Darnell. http://tellmenow.com/2014/11/national-outrage-after-no-nonsense-reporter-calls-muslims-filthy-rodents/

Continue

Exhibit 3.   A third post falsely attributed to one co-author that was formatted to appear as though he created it. Posts like these have earned users thirty-day bans, even though the users involved never created them.

Exhibit 4.   Another user was slapped for the exact same post, formatted to appear as though she created it.

We removed the post below because it doesn't follow the Facebook Community Standards:

NOTICE FROM THE ADMINISTRATIVE TEAM:

ALTHOUGH WE LOVE YOUR PASSION AND RESOLVE AND VALUE YOUR COMMENTS AND OPINIONS, IN ORDER TO GROW AND SUSTAIN THIS GROUP, THE DIALOGUE HERE MUST BE ELEVATED.

This is not a Muslim hate page, as stated in our mission here. We hate the ideology of Islam and the brutality it perpetrates and condones. Yet, threats and advocating violence towards Muslims, along with profanity and derogatory terms like Muzzies, goat f*ck'rs, shoot 'em all, kill them, etc., do not help to educate or establish and enhance credibility.

These types of posts and terms only detract from our ability to effectively raise awareness and attract those who are wavering on both sides of the fence and are seeking the truth. After all, this is what it's all about - growing our alliances and expanding our base. Some of the posts and comments here do not elicit that; nor do they properly reflect the philosophies of our page and those for this group, and we will be painted as haters without a leg to stand on. We essentially fall right into the opposition's hands and prove their argument right.

If you are unable to elevate your dialogue, we suggest that you remain on the page to observe and learn effective strategies and skills to be more effective and less vulnerable debating your views. However, until that time, we will reserve the right to remove the comments and posts of those who don't comply. We ask for your understanding and cooperation.

Thank you!

Exhibit 5. Facebook told page administrators this picture, encouraging users to follow Facebook guidelines, violated their community standards.

Exhibit 6. A picture that circulated on Facebook depicted the beheading of Dave Gaubatz in retaliation for his book, "Muslim Mafia."

From: Fatima Khan
Sent: May 28, 2014 5:58 PM
To: Joe Newby
Subject: Re: Question about work with Facebook

Hello Joe,

I read your article and had serious concerns regarding completely fabricated and false quotes you attributed to one of our staffers. Who is your editor? I would like to speak with him/her directly.

Thanks,
Fatima

Exhibit 7.   Email from Fatima Khan, Muslim Advocates.

You can't post this because it has a blocked link

The content you're trying to share includes a link that our security systems detected to be unsafe:

http://examiner.com/article/muslim-mafia-author-muslims-working-with-facebook-to-silence-critics-of-islam

Please remove this link to continue.

If you think you're seeing this by mistake, please let us know.

Close

Exhibit 8.   Shortly after Khan's email above, Facebook falsely flagged the article as "unsafe." This happened several more times with articles mentioning Islam.

you wont be raped or killed as long u don't insult islam, then its peaceful

u understand me??? if these things didn't happend, islam wouldn't exist today, so sometimes it's neccessary to kill the kuffar and rape their women, the only thing to please god (Allah swt)

Sent from web

Exhibit 9.   This is the kind of rhetoric Mark Zuckerberg and his company allows from Muslim extremists.

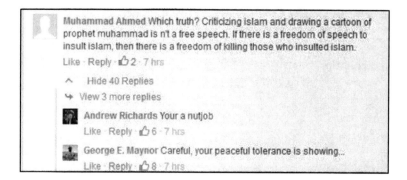

Exhibit 10.   A threat posted to Pam Geller's Facebook page. Another example of the kind of rhetoric Facebook allows.

Exhibit 11. This threatening photo of co-author Adina Kutnicki made the rounds on Facebook.

ENDNOTES

INTRODUCTION

1   Burleigh, F. W. "Was Muhammad Insane?" It's All About Muhammad RSS. March 21, 2015. http://itsallaboutmuhammad.com/2015/03/was-muhammad-insane/.

CHAPTER ONE

1   "Facebook Logo." Mark Zuckerberg. January 8, 2015. https://www.facebook.com/zuck/posts/10101844454210771.

2   David, Javier E. "Merkel Chides Facebook CEO over Hate Posts: Report." CNBC. September 27, 2015. Accessed June 28, 2016. http://www.cnbc.com/2015/09/27/angela-merkel-caught-on-hot-mic-pressing-facebook-ceo-over-anti-immigrant-posts.html.

3   Dunetz, Jeff. "EXPOSED! Facebook's Anti-Jewish Bias." The Lid. January 11, 2016. http://lidblog.com/exposed-facebooks-anti-jewish-bias/#.

4   MailOnline, Jonathan O'Callaghan for. "Is Facebook Silencing YOUR Politics? Social Media Sites Discourage Us from Voicing Our Opinions for Fear of Being Mocked." Mail Online. August 27, 2014. http://www.dailymail.co.uk/sciencetech/article-2734758/Study-Social-media-users-shy-away-opinions.html#ixzz49UdsKLPx.

5   Watson, Paul Joseph. "Facebook Refuses to Remove "Assassinate Donald Trump" Page." Infowars. March 3,

2016. http://www.infowars.com/facebook-refuses-to-remove-assassinate-donald-trump-page/.

6   Sherman, Eliezer. "Ex-IDF Intel Chief: 'State of Facebook' Greatest Mideast Threat to Israel." Algemeinercom RSS. January 31, 2016. http://www.algemeiner. com/2016/01/31/ex-idf-intel-chief-state-of-facebook-greatest-mideast-threat-to-israel/#.

CHAPTER TWO

1   Kutnicki, Adina. "The Opening of Jihad on US Soil." Arutz Sheva. November 25, 2005. http://www.israelnationalnews.com/Articles/Article.aspx/5798.

2   Kutnicki, Adina. "Articles: Terrorist Cop." Articles: Terrorist Cop. Accessed October 23, 2010. http://www.americanthinker.com/2010/10/terror_cop.html#ixzz3vUoyUvWx.

3   Muhammad Hisham Kabbani, and Seraj Hendricks. "ISCA." Jihad: A Misunderstood Concept from Islam. Accessed June 29, 2016. http://islamicsupremecouncil.org/understanding-islam/legal-rulings/5-jihad-a-misunderstood-concept-from-islam.html?start=9.

4   Bachner, Wolff. "ISIS, Islam and Obama: Understanding The Threat To The Free World [Opinion]." The Inquisitr News. September 3, 2014. http://www.inquisitr.com/1448836/isis-islam-and-obama-understanding-the-threat-to-the-free-world-special-report/#BKibu2y4hQIA7q6z.99.

5   Withnall, Adam. "Saudi Arabia executes 'a person every two days' as rate of beheadings soars under King Salman." The Independent. August 25, 2015. http://www.independent.co.uk/news/world/middle-east/saudi-arabia-executions-amnesty-international-beheadings-death-sentences-rate-under-king-salman-10470456.html.

6   "The Muslim Brotherhood's "General Strategic Goal" for North America - Discover the Networks." The Muslim

Brotherhood's "General Strategic Goal" for North America - Discover the Networks. Accessed May 29, 2016. http://www.discoverthenetworks.org/viewSubCategory. asp?id=1235.

7 Eidelberg, Prof. Paul. "America's Deadliest Enemy" Accessed May 29, 2016. https://adinakutnicki.files. wordpress.com/2012/07/islam_and_blood.pdf.

8 "Human Resources and Organizational Management." What Is the Marines' Hymn? Accessed August 04, 2016. http://www.hqmc.marines.mil/hrom/New-Employees/About-the-Marine-Corps/Hymn/.

9 "Religion in Lebanon." Wikipedia. Accessed August 04, 2016. https://en.wikipedia.org/wiki/Religion_in_Lebanon.

10 Kutnicki, Adina. "Islamic Money/Gold Laundering In Massachusetts Finances Jihad:Feds Ignore Evidence! What Can Be Done? Commentary by Adina Kutnicki." Adina Kutnicki. May 08, 2015. http://adinakutnicki. com/2015/05/08/islamic-moneygold-laundering-in-massachusetts-finances-jihadfeds-ignore-evidence-what-can-be-done-commentary-by-adina-kutnicki/.

CHAPTER THREE

1 "Digital Journalism." Wikipedia. Accessed May 27, 2016. https://en.wikipedia.org/wiki/Digital_journalism.

2 Huston, Warner Todd. "Democrats Push for New Heavy Regulations on Internet Postings, Drudge, and Blogs - Breitbart." Breitbart News. October 25, 2014. http://www.breitbart.com/big-government/2014/10/25/democrats-push-for-new-heavy-regulations-on-internet-postings-drudge-and-blogs/.

3 Boyer, Peter J. "Under Fowler, F.C.C. Treated TV as Commerce." The New York Times. January 18, 1987.

http://www.nytimes.com/1987/01/19/arts/under-fowler-fcc-treated-tv-as-commerce.html.

4   Tordjman, Jeremy. "Culture Clash Breaks Up Marriage of Old, New Media." Yahoo! News. January 12, 2016. http://news.yahoo.com/culture-clash-breaks-marriage-old-media-232403704.html.

5   Kutnicki, Adina. "Articles: Bringing Down America: A Review." Articles: Bringing Down America: A Review. April 2, 2013. http://www.americanthinker.com/2013/04/bringing_down_america_a_review.html#ixzz3w6VTPK5T.

6   "Iranian Nuclear Deal." House of Bribes: How the United States Led the Way to a Nuclear Iran. Accessed May 28, 2016. http://usatransnationalreport.org/iran-lobby/.

7   Dunetz, Jeff. "Obama Adviser Ben Rhodes Explains: He's The "Ventriloquist" To Mainstream Media's Dummies - The Lid." The Lid. May 06, 2016. http://lidblog.com/obama-advisor-ben-rhodes-explains-hes-the-ventriloquist-to-mainstream-medias-dummies/#.

8   Fredericks, Bob. "This Skilled Storyteller Duped America into Passing Iran Deal." New York Post. May 06, 2016. http://nypost.com/2016/05/06/this-skilled-storyteller-duped-america-into-passing-iran-deal/.

9   Nunez, Michael. "Former Facebook Workers: We Routinely Suppressed Conservative News." Gizmodo. May 09, 2016. http://gizmodo.com/former-facebook-workers-we-routinely-suppressed-conser-1775461006.

10 10. "Facebook Caught Censoring Conservatives, Drawing Backlash." TeaPartyFWD. May 11, 2016. Accessed July 01, 2016. http://teapartyfwd.com/actions/facebook-conservative-backlash#sthash.y2IRHcXc.dpuf.

11 "Facebook Bias: It's Baked into the Algorithms." WND. May 15, 2016. http://www.wnd.com/2016/05/facebook-

bias-its-baked-into-the-algorithms/#9jqLAHuf161Ytu
CE.99.

12 Birchall, Guy. "Zuckerberg and the Facebook Thoughtpolice." Spiked. March 4, 2016. http://www. spiked-online.com/newsite/article/zuckerberg-and-the-facebook-thoughtpolice/#.V0Mo9Pl96Un.

CHAPTER FOUR

1 Newby, Joe. "Questions Raised after Facebook Yanks Popular 'Uncle Sam's Misguided Children'" Examiner. com. July 12, 2013. http://www.examiner.com/article/ questions-raised-after-facebook-yanks-popular-uncle-sams-misguided-children.

2 Newby, Joe. "Facebook Bans Owner of Pro-veteran Page for Being 'insensitive'." Conservative Firing Line. September 19, 2015. http://conservativefiringline.com/facebook-bans-owner-of-pro-veteran-page-for-being-insensitive/.

3 Newby, Joe. "Facebook Yanks, Restores Anti-Islam Page after Admins Receive Death Threats." Examiner.com. May 21, 2014. http://www.examiner.com/article/facebook-yanks-restores-anti-islam-page-after-admins-receive-death-threats.

4 Newby, Joe. "Facebook Backs down after Unpublishing Page for British Political Party." Conservative Firing Line. December 02, 2015. http://conservativefiringline. com/facebook-backs-down-after-unpublishing-page-for-british-political-party/.

5 "Czech Anti-Islam Facebook Page Blocked." Prague Monitor. January 12, 2016. http://praguemonitor. com/2016/01/12/czech-anti-islam-facebook-page-blocked.

6 "Facebook: Stop Censoring Arab Ex-Muslims and Freethinkers NOW." Council of ExMuslims of Britain.

February 20, 2016. http://ex-muslim.org.uk/2016/02/facebook-stop-censoring-arab-ex-muslims-and-freethinkers-now/.

7 "International Covenant on Civil and Political Rights." International Covenant on Civil and Political Rights. Accessed August 04, 2016. http://www.ohchr.org/en/professionalinterest/pages/ccpr.aspx.

8 Murphy, Paul. "Blog: Blasphemy Law Comes to Facebook." Blog: Blasphemy Law Comes to Facebook. June 27, 2013. http://www.americanthinker.com/blog/2013/06/blasphemy_law_comes_to_facebook.html.

9 Newby, Joe. "Facebook: Page Advocating the Beheading of Infidels Does Not Violate Rules." Examiner.com. June 26, 2013. http://www.examiner.com/article/facebook-page-advocating-the-beheading-of-infidels-does-not-violate-rules.

10 Spencer, Robert. "Good News: "Behead Those Who Disrespect Our Prophet P.B.U.H" Has a Facebook Page!" Jihad Watch. June 25, 2013. http://www.jihadwatch.org/2013/06/good-news-behead-those-who-disrespect-our-prophet-pbuh-has-a-facebook-page.html.

11 Collins, Christopher. "Islamic Jihadist Propaganda Facebook Page Uncovered." Examiner.com. June 26, 2013. http://www.examiner.com/article/islamic-jihadist-propaganda-facebook-page-uncovered.

12 "Iranian Facebook Page Seeks Young Muslim Men 18-35 For Jihad In Syria | The Cyber & Jihad Lab." The Cyber Jihad Lab. December 10, 2015. http://cjlab.memri.org/lab-projects/tracking-jihadi-terrorist-use-of-social-media/iranian-facebook-page-seeks-young-muslim-men-18-35-for-jihad-in-syria/.

13 Shoebat, Walid. "Shoebat Exclusive: Shocking Facebook of the Canada Train Terrorist." Walid Shoebat. April 23,

2013. http://shoebat.com/2013/04/24/shoebat-exclusive-shocking-facebook-of-the-canada-train-terrorist/.

14 Unruh, Bob. "Supremes Asked to Shut down Facebook Jihad." WND. September 30, 2014. Accessed May 29, 2016. http://www.wnd.com/2014/09/supremes-asked-to-shut-down-facebook-jihad/.

CHAPTER FIVE

1   Newby, Joe. "Female Conservative Says Facebook Dismissed Death Threats, Threats of Rape." Examiner.com. August 29, 2013. http://www.examiner.com/article/female-conservative-says-facebook-dismissed-death-threats-threats-of-rape.

2   Newby, Joe. "Pamela Geller: Muslim Posted Death Threat on Facebook Page." Conservative Firing Line. February 21, 2016. http://conservativefiringline.com/pamela-geller-muslim-posted-death-threat-on-facebook-page/.

3   Geller, Pamela. "Geller: The Foes of Free Speech Are Closing In." Breitbart News. March 16, 2016. http://www.breitbart.com/london/2016/03/16/geller-the-foes-of-free-speech-are-closing-in-2/.

4   Avni, Micah Lakin. "Mark Zuckerberg Assures Muslims: Facebook a Safe Environment for You." The Blogs The Times of Israel Mark Zuckerberg Assures Muslims Facebook a Safe Environment for You Comments. December 10, 2015. http://blogs.timesofisrael.com/mark-zuckerberg-assures-muslims-facebook-a-safe-environment-for-you/.

5   Higbee, Faye. "Is Facebook Using Forgery in Jihad against Anti-terror Conservatives?" Conservative Firing Line. January 01, 2016. http://conservativefiringline.com/is-facebook-using-forgery-in-jihad-against-anti-terror-conservatives/.

6   Collins, Christopher. "Radical Muslims Post Bounty on Bloggers, Facebook Users." Examiner.com. June 27, 2013.

Accessed 2016. http://www.examiner.com/article/radical-muslims-post-bounty-on-bloggers-facebook-users.

7   June 7, 2014. http://www.barenakedislam.com/2014/06/07/this-is-what-muslims-post-about-us-on-facebook-and-their-accounts-dont-get-taken-down/.

8   Newby, Joe. "Facebook Bans Conservative for Photo of San Bernardino Shooter Tashfeen Malik." Examiner.com. December 11, 2015. http://www.examiner.com/article/facebook-bans-conservative-for-photo-of-san-bernardino-shooter-tashfeen-malik.

9   Nal, Renee. "Exclusive: Activists Increasingly Accuse Facebook of Bias against Conservatives." Examiner.com. December 09, 2015. http://www.examiner.com/article/exclusive-activists-increasingly-accuse-facebook-of-bias-against-conservatives.

10   "Facebook Cracking Down On Conservative Right, Jan Morgan Blocked From FB - Countdown To Closing Bell." YouTube. December 08, 2015. https://www.youtube.com/watch?v=y6aOveOAhmc.

11   Newby, Joe. "Facebook to User: Profane Threat of Violence, Death Does Not Violate Community Standards." Conservative Firing Line. January 02, 2016. http://conservativefiringline.com/facebook-to-user-profane-threat-of-violence-death-does-not-violate-community-standards/.

12   Goins-Phillips, Tré. "FBI Investigating Incident of Bacon Wrapped on Mosque Doors as Possible Hate Crime." The Blaze. December 30, 2015. http://www.theblaze.com/stories/2015/12/30/fbi-investigating-incident-of-bacon-wrapped-on-mosque-doors-as-possible-hate-crime/.

13   Newby, Joe. "Facebook Bans Blogger for Post Defending Victims of Migrant Rape." Conservative Firing Line. January 13, 2016. http://conservativefiringline.com/

facebook-bans-blogger-for-post-defending-victims-of-migrant-rape/.

14 "Facebook Censors Michael Savage Post of Muslims Protesting." WND. December 10, 2015. http://www.wnd.com/2015/12/facebook-censors-michael-savage-post-of-muslims-protesting/.

CHAPTER SIX

1 Newby, Joe. "'Muslim Mafia' Author: Muslims Working with Facebook to Silence Critics of Islam." Examiner.com. May 28, 2014. http://www.examiner.com/article/muslim-mafia-author-muslims-working-with-facebook-to-silence-critics-of-islam.

2 Newby, Joe. "Facebook Falsely Flags Articles Mentioning Islam as 'unsafe'" Examiner.com. May 31, 2014. http://www.examiner.com/article/facebook-falsely-flags-articles-mentioning-islam-as-unsafe.

3 Newby, Joe. "Counterterror Expert: Facebook Falsely Flags Articles, Links Critical of Islam." conservativefiringline.com. August 4, 2016.http://conservativefiringline.com/counter-terror-facebook-falsely-flags/

4 Ingram, Mathew. "Critics Say Facebook Is Erasing Pieces of History by Deleting Pages about the War in Syria." Gigaom. February 05, 2014. https://gigaom.com/2014/02/05/critics-say-facebook-is-erasing-pieces-of-history-by-deleting-pages-about-the-war-in-syria/.

5 Pizzi, Michael. "The Syrian Opposition Is Disappearing From Facebook." The Atlantic. February 4, 2014. http://www.theatlantic.com/international/archive/2014/02/the-syrian-opposition-is-disappearing-from-facebook/283562/.

6 McMahon, Felim. "Great Article Here Documenting a Disturbing Phenomenon That Has Seen Scores Of..." Great

Article Here Documenting a Disturbing Phenomenon That Has Seen Scores Of... February 4, 2014. https://plus.google.com/u/0/101449294306801004435/posts/j9DUXA68Gd5.

7   Ellefson, Lindsey. "Facebook Begins Campaign to Purge Europe of Xenophobic, Extremist Posts." Mediaite Facebook Begins Campaign to Purge Europe of Xenophobic Extremist Posts Comments. January 18, 2016. http://www.mediaite.com/online/facebook-begins-campaign-to-purge-europe-of-xenophobic-extremist-posts/.

8   Newby, Joe. "Facebook Executive, Girl Scouts Seek to Ban 'bossy' from Vocabulary." Examiner.com. March 10, 2014. http://www.examiner.com/article/facebook-executive-girl-scouts-seek-to-ban-bossy-from-vocabulary.

9   Bokhari, Allum. "Facebook Has Become The World's Most Dangerous Censor." Breitbart News. January 19, 2016. http://www.breitbart.com/tech/2016/01/19/cracking-down-on-criticism-of-refugee-atrocities-facebook-has-become-the-worlds-most-dangerous-censor/.

CHAPTER SEVEN

1   "Facebook vs. ISIS: Inside the tech giant's antiterror strategy." Engineer Marine Skipper. January 29, 2016. https://mustaphabarki2014.wordpress.com/category/facebook-has-set-up-what-amounts-to-its-own-counterterrorism-squad/

2   Hunt, Elle. "'Facebook Thinks I'm a Terrorist': Woman Named Isis Has Account Disabled." The Guardian. November 18, 2015. http://www.theguardian.com/technology/2015/nov/18/facebook-thinks-im-a-terrorist-woman-named-isis-has-account-disabled.

3   "Facebook's Anti-terror Plan: Free Adverts for Counter Extremists." WIRED UK. February 12, 2016. http://

www.wired.co.uk/news/archive/2016-02/12/facebook-counterterrorism-adverts.

4   Webb, Sam. "EBay for Jihadis: Al-Qaeda Fighters Using FACEBOOK to Buy and Sell 'CIA Weapons' - Mirror Online." Mirror. February 24, 2016. http://www.mirror.co.uk/news/world-news/ebay-jihadis-al-qaeda-fighters-7431121.

5   Warrick, Joby. "ISIS Fighters Seem to Be Trying to Sell Sex Slaves Online." Washington Post. May 28, 2016. https://www.washingtonpost.com/world/national-security/isis-fighters-appear-to-be-trying-to-sell-their-sex-slaves-on-the-internet/2016/05/28/b3d1edea-24fe-11e6-9e7f-57890b612299_story.html?wpmm=1.

6   6. Shiloach, Gilad. "ISIS Is Looking For A Few Good Social Media Folks." Vocativ. March 17, 2016. http://www.vocativ.com/298248/isis-is-looking-for-a-few-good-social-media-folks/.

7   Kollmeyer, Barbara. "Want World Peace? Share Much More on Facebook, Mark Zuckerberg Says." MarketWatch. February 26, 2016. http://www.marketwatch.com/story/facebooks-mark-zuckerberg-touts-more-sharing-as-a-route-to-world-peace-2016-02-26.

8   Soffer, Ari. "Is Civil Defense the Way to Defeat the 'knife Intifada'?" Arutz Sheva. February 25, 2016. http://www.israelnationalnews.com/News/News.aspx/208552#.V0MyLfl96Ul.

9   "The Social Networks as a Source of Inspiration and Imitation for Terrorists: The Case Study of Two Palestinian Youths Who Carried out a Stabbing Attack in a Supermarket in the Commercial Area of Sha'ar Benyamin." Terrorism-info. February 28, 2016. http://www.terrorism-info.org.il/en/article/20966.

10 Kempinski, Yoni. "'Terror Won't Stop until We Crush Their Hope'" Arutz Sheva. January 31, 2016. http://

www.israelnationalnews.com/News/News.aspx/207309#. V0M8evl96Ul.

11 "'Zuckerberg, Don't Kill Us' - Israeli NGO Blasts Facebook for Allowing Palestinian Incitement." The Jerusalem Post. January 17, 2016. http://www.jpost.com/Israel-News/ Zuckerberg-dont-kill-us-Israeli-NGO-blasts-Facebook-for-allowing-Palestinian-incitement-441784.

12 Metzler, Rebekah. "Top Quotes from Hillary Clinton's Benghazi Hearings." U.S. News and World Report. January 23, 2013. http://www.usnews.com/news/ articles/2013/01/23/top-quotes-from-hillary-clintons-benghazi-hearings.

13 "The Definition of Wilf Hey." Dictionary.com. Accessed August 04, 2016. http://www.dictionary.com/browse/wilf-hey.

CHAPTER EIGHT

1 "DoeLegal Journal.": Global Litigation Rates: The US Is Not the Leader. March 29, 2011. http://doelegal.blogspot. co.il/2011/03/global-litigation-rates-us-is-not.html.

2 "Larry Klayman." Wikipedia. Accessed May 30, 2016. https://en.wikipedia.org/wiki/Larry_Klayman.

3 "Facebook and Zuckerberg Sued for $1 Billion @ FreedomWatchUSA.org." Facebook and Zuckerberg Sued for $1 Billion @ FreedomWatchUSA.org. March 31, 2011. http://www.freedomwatchusa.org/facebook-and-zuckerberg-sued-for-1-billion.

4 Klayman v. Zuckerberg (United States Court of Appeals for the District of Columbia Circuit June 13, 2014).

5 "Federal Government Authorizes Facebook, Twitter, and YouTube to Censor." American Freedom Law Center. Accessed August 05, 2016. http://www. americanfreedomlawcenter.org/press-release/federal-

government-authorizes-facebook-twitter-and-youtube-to-censor-anti-islam-speech-lawsuit-filed/.

6   "Lakin v. Facebook – Shurat HaDin." Shurat HaDin. Accessed May 30, 2016. http://israellawcenter.org/legal_action/lakin-v-facebook/.

7   Kutnicki, Adina. "Social Media's Intersection With Slaughter of Israeli (Jewish) Mother Of 6: The Nexus. Commentary By Adina Kutnicki." Adina Kutnicki. January 18, 2016. https://adinakutnicki.com/2016/01/18/social-medias-intersection-with-slaughter-of-israeli-jewish-mother-of-6-the-nexus-commentary-by-adina-kutnicki/.

8   "Shurat HaDin Wins Major Victory in Landmark Case against Palestinian Authority." The 5 Towns Jewish Times. November 20, 2014. http://5tjt.com/ny-court-rules-sets-us-terror-victims-case-for-trial-against-palestinian-authority/.

9   "Kim v. North Korea – Shurat HaDin." Shurat HaDin. Accessed May 30, 2016. http://israellawcenter.org/legal_action/kim-v-north-korea/.

10 Klayman, Larry. "Stopping Zuckerberg's 'terrorism Network'." WND. September 12, 2014. http://www.wnd.com/2014/09/stopping-zuckerbergs-terrorism-network/#VhqFKkaO1Vh0uRf6.99.

11 Newby, Joe. "Video: White House Spokesman Suggests Suing Social Media Sites That Censor Conservatives." Conservative Firing Line. March 05, 2016. http://conservativefiringline.com/video-white-house-spokesman-suggests-suing-social-media-sites-that-censor-conservatives/.

12 Al Qahtani, Muhammad Sa'eed. "Hijrah: Migration for the Cause of Allah." Hijrah: Migration for the Cause of Allah. Accessed May 30, 2016. http://www.missionislam.com/knowledge/hijrah.htm.

13 Starnes, Todd. "Christian Bakers Fined $135,000 for Refusing to Make Wedding Cake for Lesbians | Fox News." Fox News. July 03, 2015. http://www.foxnews.com/opinion/2015/07/03/christian-bakers-fined-135000-for-refusing-to-make-wedding-cake-for-lesbians.html.

CHAPTER NINE

1 "Facebook Inc." Opensecrets RSS. Accessed May 30, 2016. http://www.opensecrets.org/pacs/lookup2.php?strID=C00502906.

2 "Facebook Inc." Opensecrets RSS. Accessed August 05, 2016. http://www.opensecrets.org/pacs/lookup2.php?strID=C00502906.

3 Trujillo, Mario. "Zuckerberg, Facebook Increasingly in Political Spotlight." TheHill. April 22, 2016. http://thehill.com/policy/technology/277183-zuckerberg-facebook-increasingly-in-political-spotlight.

4 Nunez, Michael. "Senate GOP Launches Inquiry Into Facebook's News Curation." Gizmodo. May 10, 2016. http://gizmodo.com/senate-gop-launches-inquiry-into-facebook-s-news-curati-1775767018.

5 "All Info - S.2372 - 114th Congress (2015-2016): Requiring Reporting of Online Terrorist Activity Act." Congress.gov. December 8, 2015. https://www.congress.gov/bill/114th-congress/senate-bill/2372/all-info.

6 "Text - S.2372 - 114th Congress (2015-2016): Requiring Reporting of Online Terrorist Activity Act." Congress. gov. Accessed August 05, 2016. https://www.congress.gov/bill/114th-congress/senate-bill/2372/text.

7 Barton, Ethan. "Justice Dept. Had 'Powerful Case' For IRS Targeting Charges." The Daily Caller. August 04, 2016. http://dailycaller.com/2016/08/04/justice-dept-had-powerful-case-for-irs-targeting-charges/.

8   Newby, Joe. "Facebook Bans Fox News' Todd Starnes over Post Supporting NRA, Paula Deen, Jesus." Examiner.com. June 29, 2013. http://www.examiner.com/article/facebook-bans-fox-news-todd-starnes-over-post-supporting-nra-paula-deen-jesus.

9   "'Facebook, Google Are Part of the Problem in Israel's War on Terror'" The Jerusalem Post. May 22, 2016. http://www.jpost.com/Israel-News/Politics-And-Diplomacy/Erdan-Facebook-Google-are-part-of-the-problem-in-fight-against-terror-454665.

CHAPTER TEN

1   Newby, Joe. "Facebook Protest Calls for 'blackout' of Site over Treatment of Conservatives." Examiner.com. August 04, 2013. http://www.examiner.com/article/facebook-protest-calls-for-blackout-of-site-over-treatment-of-conservatives.

2   Newby, Joe. "Facebook Suspends 'Blackout' Event Admin for Post Saying Woman Seeking Attention." Examiner.com. August 08, 2013. http://www.examiner.com/article/facebook-suspends-blackout-event-admin-for-post-saying-woman-seeking-attention.

3   Cracker, Miz. "Facebook's "Real Name" Fix Isn't a Fix at All." Slate Magazine. November 04, 2015. http://www.slate.com/blogs/outward/2015/11/04/facebook_real_name_policy_the_changes_for_trans_people_drag_queens_and_others.html.

4   "Adam Smith." : The Concise Encyclopedia of Economics. Accessed August 05, 2016. http://www.econlib.org/library/Enc/bios/Smith.html.

CONCLUSION

1   Bokhari, Allum. "Facebook Has Become The World's Most Dangerous Censor." Breitbart News. January 19, 2016.

http://www.breitbart.com/tech/2016/01/19/cracking-down-on-criticism-of-refugee-atrocities-facebook-has-become-the-worlds-most-dangerous-censor/.

2   Waters, Anne-Marie. "Europe's Rape Epidemic: Western Women Will Be Sacrificed At The Altar Of Mass Migration." Breitbart News. October 06, 2015. http://www.breitbart.com/london/2015/10/06/europes-rape-epidemic-western-women-will-be-sacrificed-at-the-alter-of-mass-migration/.

3   "The Quotations Page: Quote from Albert Einstein." The Quotations Page. Accessed August 04, 2016. http://www.quotationspage.com/quote/26032.html.

4   Lagorio-Chafkin, Christine. "Facebook's 3 Huge Plans for the Future." Inc.com. June 17, 2016. http://www.inc.com/christine-lagorio/facebook-big-goals.html.

5   Newby, Joe. "Facebook Admits: 'Rogue Employees' May Be behind Censorship of Conservatives." Examiner.com. May 25, 2016. http://www.examiner.com/article/facebook-admits-rogue-employees-may-be-behind-censorship-of-conservatives.

6   "Texas Ranger Hall of Fame." The Official Texas Ranger Hall of Fame and Museum in Waco, Texas. Accessed August 04, 2016. http://www.texasranger.org/halloffame/McDonald_Jesse.htm.

AFTERWORD

1   Rappaport, Mike. "Did the FBI Fail and Is It Failing to Admit It? - Online Library of Law & Liberty." Online Library of Law Liberty. June 14, 2016. http://www.libertylawsite.org/2016/06/14/did-the-fbi-fail-and-are-they-failing-to-admit-it/.

2   "US Intelligence Misses Cues to Terror - Again." June 13, 2016. Accessed June 27, 2016. http://www.debka.com/article/25479/US-intelligence-misses-cues-to-terror---again.

3   Zimmerman, Malia. "Orlando Terrorist's Chilling Facebook Posts from Inside Club Revealed." *Fox News* (Fox News), June 15, 2016. http://www.foxnews.com/us/2016/06/15/orlando-terrorists-chilling-facebook-posts-from-inside-club-revealed.html.

4   "Paris Attacks: Father of Victim Sues Twitter, Facebook and Google over ISIS Accounts." CBSNews. June 15, 2016. http://www.cbsnews.com/news/paris-attacks-victim-sues-twitter-facebook-google-youtube-isis-nohemi-gonzalez/.

5   Newby, Joe. "Facebook Bans Pam Geller, Removes 'Stop Islamization' Group in Wake of Orlando Attack." June 12, 2016. Accessed June 27, 2016. http://conservativefiringline.com/facebook-bans-pam-geller-removes-stop-islamization-group-wake-orlando-attack/.

6   Campbell, Andy. "Facebook Will Fight for Rights Of Muslims, Zuckerberg Vows." Huffington Post. December 9, 2015.

INDEX

CPSIA information can be obtained
at www.ICGtesting.com
Printed in the USA
LVOW10s0308081116
512078LV00001B/33/P